THE PEANUTS™ ILLUSTRATED SONGBOOK

With an Introduction by
Hank Bordowitz

HAL•LEONARD® CORPORATION
7777 W. Bluemound Rd. P.O. Box 13819 Milwaukee, WI 53213

Photographs courtesy of David Guaraldi (p. 4, 11),
Lee Mendelson Film Productions, Inc. (p. 7, 9, 13, 18)
and Bill Melendez Productions (p. 8)

ISBN 0-634-03090-6

Visit Peanuts™ on the Internet at
www.snoopy.com

Library of Congress cataloguing-in-publication data
has been applied for.

Visit Hal Leonard Online at
www.halleonard.com

CONTENTS

INTRODUCTION

When you think of the comic *Peanuts*, your mind's eye probably offers up an image of Snoopy on his doghouse, either lying on top or dressed in World War I Flying Ace drag. Or Charlie Brown bowled over by someone getting a piece of his fastball or Lucy snatching away the football he's trying to kick. Or Linus, dragging his blanket behind him. Or any number of other images that have turned into cultural touchstones of the twentieth century from the universally beloved strip the late Charles Schulz drew for fifty years.

But if you *hear* anything when you think of *Peanuts*, chances are it's not the ubiquitous Beethoven sonatas Schroeder plays (the music notation in the strip, by the way, is entirely accurate). Almost certainly, when you hear a soundtrack to *Peanuts*, the music Vince Guaraldi created for the animated specials is dancing in your head.

"His music is very much a part of the fabric of American culture," Grammy-winning, multi-platinum pianist George Winston said when he recorded an album of this music, *Linus and Lucy—The Music of Vince Guaraldi,* in 1996. "His music generates joy, warmth and humor, as well as whimsical feelings." Winston's version of Guaraldi's music shipped gold and has since sold three quarters of a million copies.

Vince Guaraldi

Some of Vince Guaraldi's best music became inextricably associated with *Peanuts,* and the pieces and arrangements he created became nearly as indelible as the images from the strip. Guaraldi scored the first fifteen of the animated specials and the 1970 film *A Boy Named Charlie Brown,* and every subsequent *Peanuts* animation used elements of Guaraldi's music.

"Without his music," Guaraldi's son David posits, "the *Peanuts* TV shows wouldn't be what they were."

As the music in this book illustrates, you may not know the titles, but you probably know the tunes. Through nearly four decades, "A Charlie Brown Christmas" has been the stalwart holiday special no one wants to miss. The music has become as ingrained as the image of the pathetic little Christmas tree that blooms, given a little love and some decoration. Here's how it all came about.

There are many parallels between the life of *Peanuts* creator Charles Schulz and *Peanuts* composer Vince Guaraldi. Both grew up in less than affluent families. Both served in wars. Both worked for newspapers. Both would just as soon not travel and both were obsessed with their art.

For Schulz that art was cartooning. He loved his art, although, despite exhibits of his work in the Louvre in Paris, the Smithsonian in Washington D.C., the Montreal Museum of Fine Arts and other museums around the globe, to his dying day he would claim the form never got the respect it deserved.

The son of a barber who survived on an endless series of 35-cent haircuts, he was born and spent most of his first forty years in Minneapolis. He and his father (who had left school after the third grade) shared a mutual love of the comics that brought all four local papers into the Schulz household every day. By the time he went to school, Schulz was drawing Popeye and other characters. He had his first piece of art published in the *Ripley's Believe It or Not* comic when he was fifteen. He served during the last two years of World War II, rising to the rank of Staff Sergeant.

After the war, he took a course at a local art correspondence school and wound up working there as an instructor. He also started doing various graphic arts chores, lettering comics for the Catholic magazine *Timeless Topix*, selling the occasional drawing to the *Saturday Evening Post* and doing a weekly panel called *Li'l Folks* for the *St. Paul Pioneer Press.* He started sending the *Press* panel around to syndicates. After a while, he negotiated a deal with United Features for a strip version. Because *Li'l Folks* sounded too much like *Li'l Abner*, United Features changed the name of the strip to *Peanuts*, signifying the little people at the heart of the comic. Schulz never really liked the title, and would have preferred to call it *Good Ol' Charlie Brown*, but he didn't have much say as a syndicate novice. The first strip appeared in seven newspapers on October 2, 1950. The first year, Schulz earned ninety dollars a week in royalties.

From the beginning, the strip was unique. Schulz drew it from the perspective of his young characters. Adults weren't allowed. "They just wouldn't fit into the frame," Schulz would explain. Rather than basing the strip on a series of gags, he based it on the interactions of a group of characters. Their personalities and idiosyncrasies interlocked to become the backbone of the strip. As one observer noted, the fifty-year run of *Peanuts* represented "arguably the longest story ever told by one human being, longer than any epic poem, any Tolstoy novel, any Wagner opera."

His work attracted much academic attention over the years. Author and aesthetic philosopher Umberto Eco wrote extensively about how well Charlie Brown reflected a society that seeks "salvation through the routine formulas suggested to him by…the art of making friends, culture in four easy lessons, the pursuit of happiness." *Peanuts* became the topic of two best-selling books on theology, *The Gospel According to Peanuts* and *The*

Parables of Peanuts. Noted popular culture theorist Arthur Asa Berger proclaimed Snoopy "an existential hero in *every sense* of the term, [a dog that] strives...to overcome what seems to be his fate—that he is a dog."

All this struck Schulz as a bit highfalutin' for a comic strip. He always maintained that he merely sought to entertain.

Vince Guaraldi discusses a score with John Scott Trotter, who arranged and conducted much of Guaraldi's music for the Peanuts *animated specials.*

Music played an important role in the strip, both as content and in its progress. In 1951, Schulz introduced the character Schroeder, who sat down at a toy piano and started pounding out Beethoven. Schulz, a classical music aficionado, would explain that he much preferred Brahms. "I could listen to him all day," he once said. "But Brahms isn't a funny word, Beethoven is."

"I remember one of the few times I saw a teardrop from him," recalls Lee Mendelson, who produced all of the Charlie Brown cartoons. "I had been to Vienna. There's a small courtyard where eight or ten of the most famous composers are buried. I went and put a little Snoopy pin on Beethoven's grave. A little Austrian girl came up and said, *'Warum nicht Schroeder?'* [Why not Schroeder?] I had a little Schroeder pin in the car, so I put that on the grave. When I told Schulz that, a tear came to his eye. It was a strange, emotional moment."

Schulz would painstakingly copy actual measures of Beethoven piano scores into the strip when Schroeder played his toy piano. This attention to detail and the classical music context caught the attention of an editor at New York book publisher Rinehart. He approached Schulz and United Features about republishing the comic strip in books. These books helped expand the reach of the comic strip.

Within three years, *Peanuts* started catching on in a big way. Schulz was earning $30,000 a year for the strip (a princely wage in 1953). Two years later, he earned the recognition of his peers, receiving his first Reuben Award as outstanding cartoonist of 1955. With the growing recognition of the strips and the characters (to the point that people realized there was no character named "Peanuts" in the strip), other opportunities knocked. Toy statues of Charlie Brown and Snoopy were licensed. Kodak struck a deal to use the characters for a camera handbook. In 1957, the advertising firm of J. Walter Thompson approached him about using the characters in animated commercials for the Ford Falcon. These cartoons introduced Schulz to animator Bill Melendez. Melendez had started his own production house after a career that had already spanned *Pinocchio* and *Looney Tunes*.

Charles Schulz and Bill Melendez play out the Lucy and Charlie Brown football gag.

"We did a lot of them," Melendez recalls of the Ford ads. "A few every year for several years. Ever since we had a very wonderful relationship. He once called me up and said, 'Bill, I'm a strip artist and that's what I do every day, and you're an animator and that's what you do every day. I'll do my strip and you animate.' That gave me tremendous freedom and tremendous responsibilities."

By 1963, Charles M. Schulz had drawn *Peanuts* for some thirteen years. He had relocated from Minneapolis to the Bay Area not too long before. He would have gladly stayed in Minneapolis, his hometown, but he "had a restless wife." So they set up housekeeping in Sebastopol, a San Francisco suburb.

Not far from Sebastopol, after years of making television documentaries, Lee Mendelson had just started his own production house. His first network documentary on baseball legend Willie Mays had earned a modicum of success. Shortly after finishing it, he was reading the comics and saw

Charlie Brown striking out for the umpteenth time. It occurred to him that he had just made a documentary about the world's greatest baseball player, why not follow it with one on the world's worst—Charlie Brown? He approached Schulz with the idea. The normally shy cartoonist was also a big sports fan and had seen Mendelson's Willie Mays documentary. He agreed.

Lee Mendelson, Bill Melendez and Charles Schulz.

By 1962, Mendelson needed an inspiration. The documentary on Schulz was going well. Mostly live action, it covered how Schulz worked, his inspirations. It also included a short piece of animation, done by Melendez. As he drove home that day in 1962, he pondered what to do about the soundtrack for that piece of film.

He could go any number of ways. If he asked Schulz, they probably would have gone with Brahms. He might have opted for one of the more standard composers doing film music. Mendelson didn't really think any of them captured the whimsical spirit of his subject. He was leaning toward jazz. He started asking around, half jokingly, about jazz musicians who had kids and might just read *Peanuts*. He solicited local musicians Dave Brubeck and Cal Tjader as to whether they could do it, but both were too busy. Tjader mentioned the name of a pianist he had worked with over the years, a local Bay Area player named Vince Guaraldi.

He mused over this as he drove across the Golden Gate Bridge, casually observing the sailboats at play in the bay. He had an affinity for this bridge he crossed pretty nearly every day—the first documentary he ever made was on the history of the bridge. As he crossed, the answer to his quandary breezed through his car radio. He heard, for the first time, a winsome bit of jazz called "Cast Your Fate to the Wind." And he knew he had found the sound he sought. The recording was by Vince Guaraldi.

"I called Ralph Gleason, who was jazz editor, at the time, for the *San Francisco Chronicle*," Mendelson recalls. Gleason told Mendelson, "I just had lunch with him."

Vince Guaraldi had lived in the Bay Area all his life. He stood only 5'2", wore black-rimmed glasses, and had a huge handlebar moustache that became one of his physical trademarks. He grew up in a single parent home, but one that was filled with music. Two of his uncles were professional players, one working in the band for Art Linkletter's *House Party*, another playing violin and fronting an orchestra at a local hot spot. At Lincoln High School, his main claim to fame was playing great boogie-woogie piano. Upon graduation, he was drafted into the Korean conflict.

After his hitch in Korea, he played piano casually and apprenticed at the *San Francisco Daily News* until an accident nearly cost him a finger. When he recovered, he was determined to play music full time. He started taking classes at the San Francisco Conservatory of Music and landed the piano seat in a band led by former Thelonious Monk sax player Kermit Scott. In 1950, he began working with vibraharpist Cal Tjader.

"He was very much influenced by Bud Powell in that early period and he had tremendous drive," Tjader would recall. "He comped with his left hand like Powell and played a lot of single note melodies with speed and agility in his right hand."

Throughout the '50s, Guaraldi worked with Tjader, with whom he made his first appearance on record with *Vibraharp* in 1953. He also played with trombonist Bill Harris and bassist Chubby Jackson. In the mid and late '50s he toured with Woody Herman's Thundering Herd. With the legendary jazz big band, Guaraldi had the opportunity to play Carnegie Hall (a personal ambition) and see the world.

Beyond being a respected player, Guaraldi became a prolific composer. "He just sat down at the Steinway and wrote," his son David recalls. "I don't know what went on in his brain. He was always writing. He would get up at four in the morning and write."

The Vince Guaraldi Trio in 1962, with Vince Guaraldi on piano, Monty Budwig on bass, and Colin Bailey on drums.

At the turn of the decade, he left Herman and started to put together the first in a series of mercurial trios. He had picked up on the Latin music that had not infiltrated the West Coast Cool jazz scene, but was very big nearly everywhere else. He also learned some of the bossa nova rhythms that were wafting in from Brazil. All of these became a part of his music. He became a fixture around the Bay Area, recording for the local label, a small jazz and poetry oriented company called Fantasy Records. In their first decade in business, the company's most successful sellers had been sides by comedian Lenny Bruce, though they also had records by John Coltrane, Allen Ginsberg, Miles Davis and numerous others in their catalogue.

Guaraldi recorded with guitarist Bola Sete, adding to his Brazilian chops. He became something of a local hero, and while the territory he covered with his own trio was just a small swath of the Bay and Capital areas, from Monterey to Concord, he was pretty happy with that, made a living, supported his family, and periodically went to the lean-to behind Fantasy's offices on Treat Street, or one of the local radio station studios in San Francisco, to record. In 1962, his interest in the music of Brazil led him to pick up on Antonio Carlos Jobim's soundtrack to the Oscar-winning film *Black Orpheus*.

"The first thing I did with him," recalls drummer Colin Bailey, "was *Jazz Impressions of Black Orpheus.* That was in February of 1962. We recorded that at KQED from midnight until four in the morning. We were playing that stuff out all the time, so we just went in there and did it."

One of the tracks they recorded that morning was an original composition Guaraldi had been playing for years. "I'll tell you when I wrote it," he says to Ralph Gleason in the T.V. special made about the record, *Anatomy of a Hit*. "I think it was in '58, just about when I left Cal. In fact, I brought it to Cal, but I never played it until after I left Woody, when I was at the Outside At The Inside in Palo Alto...Every time I play the tune I really get a reaction."

"People loved that immediately," Bailey concurs, "even before it was recorded. We played it a couple of times a night."

Fantasy released the song, "Cast Your Fate to the Wind," as the b-side of the first single from the album, Guaraldi's take on Jobim's "Samba De Orpheus." While the Jobim track didn't set radio on fire, a local DJ in Sacramento fell in love with the b-side and started playing it. The song lit up the switchboard and started spreading from station to station. Suddenly, Guaraldi found himself mingling on the charts with the likes of Elvis Presley, Dion and The Shirelles, as "Cast Your Fate to the Wind" became that most rare of jazz tracks to reach the Top 40, peaking at 22. That year it won the Grammy Award for Best Original Jazz Composition.

When the single hit, he moved his family from Westlake, over the Golden Gate to Mill Valley in Marin County. "Everything about life changed completely," is how David Guaraldi summed up the effect of the song on his father's family and career.

Gleason put Mendelson in contact with Guaraldi. Guaraldi, as it turned out, was a big *Peanuts* fan. Like Schulz and his father, Guaraldi enjoyed the comic with his kids David and Dia, who at the time were just around the same age as the kids in the strip. It was an offer the pianist couldn't refuse.

Not long after that, a piece of music "just came into his head while he was driving across the Golden Gate Bridge," David Guaraldi recalls. "He could just piece music together in his mind. So he comes home, real quickly, sits down and starts playing it."

"Vince called me on the phone," Mendelson adds. "He said, 'I gotta play something for you.' I said, 'I don't want to hear it on the phone, because you don't hear the highs and lows.' He said, 'I've got to play it now or I'm going to explode. I don't want to forget it.' He played 'Linus and Lucy' for the first time and I just knew instantly that it was so right and so perfect. I even remember thinking, 'This is going to make this show happen.' It was just perfect. It was like a godsend."

Lee Mendelson, Charles Schulz and Bill Melendez look over a set of storyboards.

"The minute they heard 'Linus and Lucy' they said 'Let's go!'" recalls David Guaraldi. "And still, I think my father was more excited than they were."

Ironically, the documentary didn't sell for seven years, at which point it won an Emmy. Guaraldi recorded an album based on the film, though. *Jazz Impressions of A Boy Named Charlie Brown* included "Linus and Lucy" and some of the other music he wound up writing for and around the documentary. Schulz did the cover art for the album, featuring Guaraldi sitting at Schroeder's toy piano with Charlie Brown on guitar, Linus on bass, Lucy leaning on the piano, staring at Guaraldi while Schroeder walks the other way, hands in his pockets, looking over his shoulders. Snoopy, of course, dances.

"We were stuffing Charlie Brown pictures in the albums," recalls Mendelson. "We had about 10,000 albums, it took us forever. One of the guys stuffing pictures in the albums was the accountant. I lost track of the accountant until I was watching the Oscars about ten years later and Saul Zaentz was picking up all the Oscars for *One Flew Over the Cuckoo's Nest.*"

While no one saw Mendelson's documentary on TV at the time, it had received wide viewership among advertising executives and people at the television networks. A year and a half after the film wrapped, the *Peanuts* phenomenon was in full swing. There were *Peanuts* greeting cards, *Peanuts* sweatshirts, *Peanuts* lunchboxes, plush Snoopy dolls, *Peanuts* coffee mugs, a whole range of things that had brought *Peanuts* off of the comics page and into other aspects of people's lives. Charlie Brown and the gang were even on the cover of *Time* magazine.

Mendelson got a call from one of the advertising people who had seen the film, and they asked him if he and Schulz could put together a treatment for a Christmas special in a week, and make the actual special in six months. Mendelson said, "Sure." Then he called Schulz and told him about this stroke of good fortune. With so little time to put things together, they went with what they knew, and part of that equation was the music of Vince Guaraldi.

"Vince was perfect for all of us," notes Melendez. "He was easy to work with, like Schulz. When I finished the storyboards for "A Charlie Brown Christmas" and showed him my bar sheets, the pages that show the music and dialogue cues for each scene, he'd say, 'Just tell me how many yards you want.' By yards, he meant seconds of music."

Guaraldi had kept busy, playing regularly throughout the Bay Area and even further afield on occasion. "He was really popular in the early '60s," David Guaraldi relates. "He was working like crazy."

Nonetheless, Guaraldi was more than happy to revisit his association with *Peanuts*, especially in the context of a Christmas album, which he released when the special aired. David and his younger sister Dia were still hovering around *Peanuts* age at the time and he thought it was a great idea—a jazz recording that children and parents could enjoy.

For the soundtrack, Guaraldi had rearranged versions of classic Christmas carols like "O Tannenbaum," "The Christmas Song (Chestnuts Roasting on an Open Fire)" and "What Child Is This." Additionally he wrote several other seasonal songs to fit the mood set up in the storyboard, like "Skating" and one that became a holiday standard in its own right, "Christmas Time Is Here."

"Vince had written 'Christmas Time Is Here' as an instrumental," Mendelson notes. "The show was done and I'm looking at it and it was too soft of an opening. I said, 'We've got to get somebody to write some words.' I called the Sherman Brothers [who wrote so much of the Disney Music during that period]; I called a whole bunch of people. Everyone was busy and we only had a few weeks so, I don't know why, but I had this little envelope and I wrote this little poem to the music, which became 'Christmas Time Is Here.' It's been covered, I don't know, twenty or thirty times, most recently by Vanessa Williams. It's just so funny how that evolved because it was an afterthought."

For the 1998 holiday season alone, artists ranging from Shawn Colvin, Kenny Loggins and Brian McKnight to Diana Krall and the rock band Chicago recorded versions of the song. Other artists include rock guitar star Steve Vai, R.E.M., The Beach Boys, Bob Hope, The Commodores, Grover Washington, Jr., Mel Torme (turnabout, as he wrote "The Christmas Song"), John Pizzarelli and El Vez.

Of course the score included what was to become the de facto theme music for the *Peanuts* specials, "Linus and Lucy." One of Guaraldi's best-known compositions, by sound if not by name, it says a great deal about Guaraldi as a composer and his appeal. The piece is straightforward enough that it has become a popular piece for piano method books, yet fun enough to galvanize an audience.

"When my daughter was about to have her baby last February," Mendelson recalls, "it was ten minutes before Valentine's Day. She was having a cesarean, so the doctor says, 'Hey, if you want to wait ten minutes, you can have the baby on Valentine's Day.' She says, 'Okay.' So, the doctor is standing there. He told me subsequently that he had never really stopped in the middle of a delivery before. He doesn't know what to do, so he starts to hum. Now, he doesn't know what I do or even my last name. He starts to hum 'Linus and Lucy.' When it's all done, I asked him, 'Excuse me, why were you humming that song?' He says, 'Oh, my daughter's learning it on the piano. I don't even know the name of it, but it's just kind of catchy.'"

"In school, I was known as the guy who could play Charlie Brown," recalls noted jazz pianist Cyrus Chestnut, who recorded his own version of the entire "A Charlie Brown Christmas" for the 2000 holiday season. "It all started at a Mason Dixon stage band contest at my high school. While the judges were making their decision, my band director said to me, 'Go play for the people—keep them entertained.' So, that's what I attempted to do. Everyone was kind of listening until, at one point, I just said, 'Oh what the heck' and I started playing the 'Linus and Lucy' bass line. Everybody just went up. People really liked it. Afterwards, everyone said to me, 'Hey man, are you going to play *Peanuts* today?' Any time I was at a piano, that's what I'd hear. 'Linus and Lucy' was kind of a signature piece for me throughout high school."

It has also proved to be a remarkably versatile piece. In addition to versions that accentuate the piano by Guaraldi acolytes and peers like Winston and Benoit, Dave Brubeck recorded a funky version with his sons. Wynton Marsalis recorded a version full of New Orleans spirit with his father. It became a standard in shows by the late jazzabilly guitarist Danny Gatton and the Dave Matthews Band, and was recorded as well by hard rock guitarist Gary Hoey.

Additionally, it has been used as the backdrop to commercials. Obviously, advertisements featuring the *Peanuts* characters, like those for Hallmark, would use Guaraldi music. More often than not, it would be the distinctive "Linus and Lucy." A recent spot for a car company featured "Linus and Lucy" as a dog rolled a man in a recliner down a hill. After more than thirty-five years, the piece still has legs.

There was great consternation at Mendelson Productions, Melendez Animation, CBS and the advertising agency over "A Charlie Brown Christmas". Mendelson, Melendez and Schulz had taken the creative high road in many ways. Rather than use adult actors doing kids voices, they opted to use real children. There was no laugh track (Schulz insisted). The animation was very limited. They had Linus read a good portion of the Gospel According to St. Luke, again at Schulz' insistence.

"I said, 'Sparky, we can't have that—this is religion, it just doesn't go in a cartoon,'" Mendelson recalls. "He just looked at me very coldly with his blue eyes and said, 'If we don't do it, who will? We can do it.' And he was right."

You couldn't have judged that by the two CBS vice presidents for whom they screened the show. "They didn't hide their disappointment," Mendelson remembers. "'Too slow…the kids don't sound pro…the music is all wrong…the Bible thing scares us…' I thought we had killed it."

"A Charlie Brown Christmas" preempted the enormously popular "Beverly Hillbillies". It drew 47% of all the people with televisions on that night in 1965. When it was rerun the next year it did even better, pulling in 57% of the audience. It won an Emmy Award and a George Peabody Award for excellence in children's programming. Not a little of that success is attributed to the music.

Charles Schulz accepts the Emmy for Best Network Animated Special in 1966 for A Charlie Brown Christmas, *with Lee Mendelson and Bill Melendez.*

"The thing about Vince Guaraldi," says Chestnut, "he just knew how to make those characters come to life, make the whole strip come to life. Vince and Charles Schulz and Charlie Brown, they really connected so well. The music is simple yet complex, but most of all, it's really enjoyable. You're talking about what is flat-out good music. I think Vince is one of music's unsung heroes of storytelling."

"Vince's interpretations all remind me of my own childhood," notes George Winston. "It's like a novelist. It all goes in there, grist for the mill."

"I went to school the next day," David Guaraldi recalls, "and I was like an instant hero. It was like, 'Hey, your dad did this, your dad did that.' The teachers all recognized me and from then on, I was known as Vince Guaraldi's son."

"I was twelve years old when I saw that show in 1965," Benoit notes, "and I was hooked on the music. It was jazz, not the usual singsong stuff that accompanied cartoons. It was so refreshing. There was humor and lightness. It was hip, like the characters. The music mirrored the characters."

"Without the music," Mendelson remarks, "I don't know if we would have done more than one show."

One effect Guaraldi's music for the *Peanuts* specials had that no one could have anticipated was the effect it had on jazz. "A Charlie Brown Christmas" aired in 1965. Assuming the group of youngsters watching the show were between six and twelve at the time, that would make them in their early to mid twenties in the early '80s when a large crop of younger jazz players, who became known as jazz's 'young lions,' suddenly became very evident on the scene. Could it be a coincidence or is it possible the soundtrack helped revive the flagging fortunes of jazz?

"We put it into the mainstream by putting it onto cartoons," Mendelson postulates. "We had kids hearing jazz who probably would have never heard jazz."

"I loved his soundtrack for 'A Charlie Brown Christmas,'" says George Winston, who was in his late teens when the show first ran. "The day after I saw the show, I bought the album and from then on I collected all of Vince's records."

"I remember digging the music on those Charlie Brown specials when I was just six or seven," adds Cyrus Chestnut.

"When I was a boy, the only time you would hear jazz on television was when Charlie Brown came to town, " the dean of that group of 'young lions,' Wynton Marsalis notes. "When I was growing up we always liked that music. We loved it 'cause our father knew him. That made us think our father was important."

Over the course of the next eleven years, Guaraldi wrote and played the music for sixteen more *Peanuts* specials and shared scoring chores on the first *Peanuts* feature film, *A Boy Named Charlie Brown*, with Rod McKuen in 1970.

"We were up for an Academy Award for Best Original Score for a Movie for *A Boy Named Charlie Brown*," recalls Mendelson. "Our movies had jazz in them, too. So, we got an Oscar nomination, but we had a little problem and lost to a young group that had written something called 'Let It Be.' So, we had the honor of being defeated by the Beatles in our one shot at an Oscar. We weren't too surprised."

One of the things this allowed Guaraldi was the ability to stay pretty much in one place and create, rather than do the grind of touring. "I know what it is to look at musicians and think they're glamorous," he told Gleason in the *Anatomy of a Hit* program. "At one time in my life, I felt that deeply, you know, but one trip on the road and I knew that what you think is glamour is really beat. They're not cool, man; they just can't move. All they're thinking about is: 'It's a hundred more miles before we hit the bed.'"

"Vince didn't like to tour," Winston concurs. "He stayed close to home."

"He was a private person," adds David Guaraldi. "He was just a kid from San Francisco who wanted to stay around the area. He chose what he wanted to do when he wanted to do it."

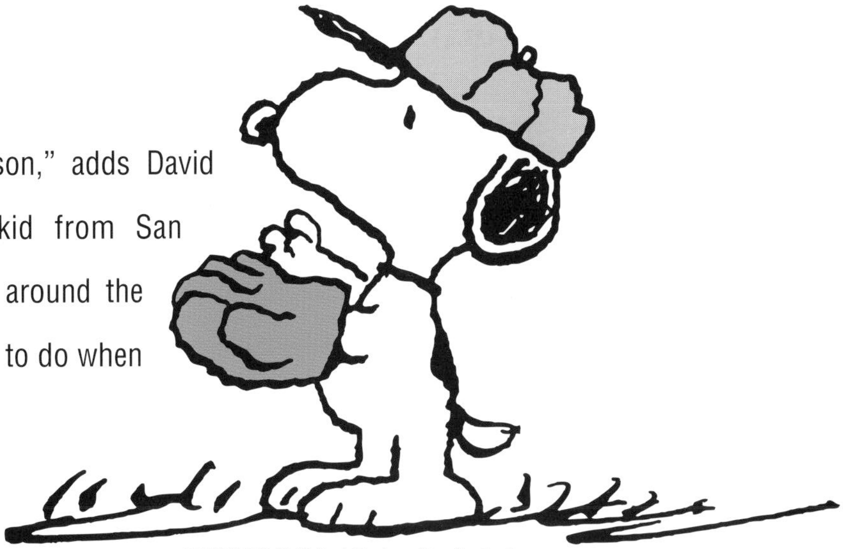

With each new show, he revisited some of the popular themes, like "Linus and Lucy," and created a few new "yards," like "Heartburn Waltz" from "A Charlie Brown Thanksgiving" and "The Great Pumpkin Waltz" from "It's the Great Pumpkin, Charlie Brown." All of the music was created to fit both the character and the scene, but also bore Guaraldi's distinctive musical stamp.

"I think Vince's music was one of the main contributions that made the Charlie Brown shows successful," Mendelson maintains. "Vince gave it a sound and individuality that no other cartoon had ever had. We received as much mail about the music as we did about any other aspect of the show."

While "Linus and Lucy" played an important role in every show, each show had its own unique musical themes. These displayed Guaraldi's personal changes as a writer and composer. The 1973 special "A Charlie Brown Thanksgiving", for example, has synthesizers, horns and electric guitar, a long way from the piano trio of the Christmas show.

"He was moving in a fusion jazz-rock direction," a member of his late '70s combo, Seward McClain, recalled to Bob Doerschuck in *Keyboard* magazine.

"He didn't just stick to one kind of music," adds David Guaraldi. "He went through different Latin phases; he started using electric instruments, taught himself how to use the guitar and recorded these things. He sang on an album. From 1955 until 1967 he recorded for Fantasy. From '68 he did three albums for Warner Brothers. That was at the height of his career. There was *Peanuts* music on these things. One of the albums was called *Oh, Good Grief.*"

Guaraldi continued to record and play music beyond the *Peanuts* pale as well. In 1976, his band enjoyed a regular gig at a club called Butterfield's. They finished their first set on February 6, 1976 with a version of the Beatles' "Eleanor Rigby," and went back to the dressing rooms. Guaraldi collapsed backstage, and his band was unable to revive him. He had died of a heart attack at the age of forty-seven.

"He had finished this Arbor Day thing, for sure, the week before he passed away," David Guaraldi recalls. "*Peanuts* carried on. They aired it, and there was a memorial thing saying he'd passed away."

Many other composers worked on the subsequent twenty-nine *Peanuts* specials and the Saturday morning cartoon, *The Charlie Brown and Snoopy Show*. But all of the soundtracks used some element of Guaraldi's music.

"We did eight shows called *This Is America, Charlie Brown,*" Mendelson says. "Wynton Marsalis did the one about the Wright Brothers, George Winston did the one about the drawing up of the Constitution and Benoit did the one about the great inventors. Brubeck did another one. When Brubeck did the show for us, he said, 'I guess I should have done the first one.' We had jazz all over the place."

This music became very well documented. Marsalis released *Joe Cool's Blues* in 1995. The album featured his regular band doing much of what he wrote for the special along with his father's trio playing music by his old acquaintance, Vince Guaraldi. Both came together for "Linus and Lucy."

Winston's tribute to Guaraldi came out around the same time. For the holiday season, 2000, Cyrus Chestnut did his own version of the music from "A Charlie Brown Christmas". Around the same time, David Benoit put out *Here's to You, Charlie Brown—50 Great Years.*

Benoit became the de facto holder of the musical franchise for *Peanuts* music in the early 1990s. "David Benoit, who I'm really friendly with, has taken the music in the last fifteen years since they've used him and kept my father's style alive with it," David Guaraldi acknowledges. "I'm sure you're aware of his music. He plays the music pretty much the same. He can't say enough about my father, and me him. There's material to do two new shows right now. They're going to do it, but it's going to take time."

The future of the *Peanuts* television shows became somewhat dicey when Charles Schulz retired at the end of 1999, finally giving in to the cancer that he had been fighting for about a year. He swore that no one else would draw *Peanuts.* On February 12, 2000, the day before his last original Sunday strip ran, Schulz succumbed to the cancer, dying in his sleep at the age of seventy-seven. While the world will see no more original *Peanuts* strips, newspapers continue to run the classics. Similarly, Mendelson has plans to make several more specials based on some of the fifty years of adventures of Charlie Brown, Snoopy and the rest of the gang.

Which, if nothing else, means Charlie Brown and Vince Guaraldi have not seen (or heard) the last of each other.

— Hank Bordowitz

BASEBALL THEME

By VINCE GUARALDI

Moderate Jazz Waltz

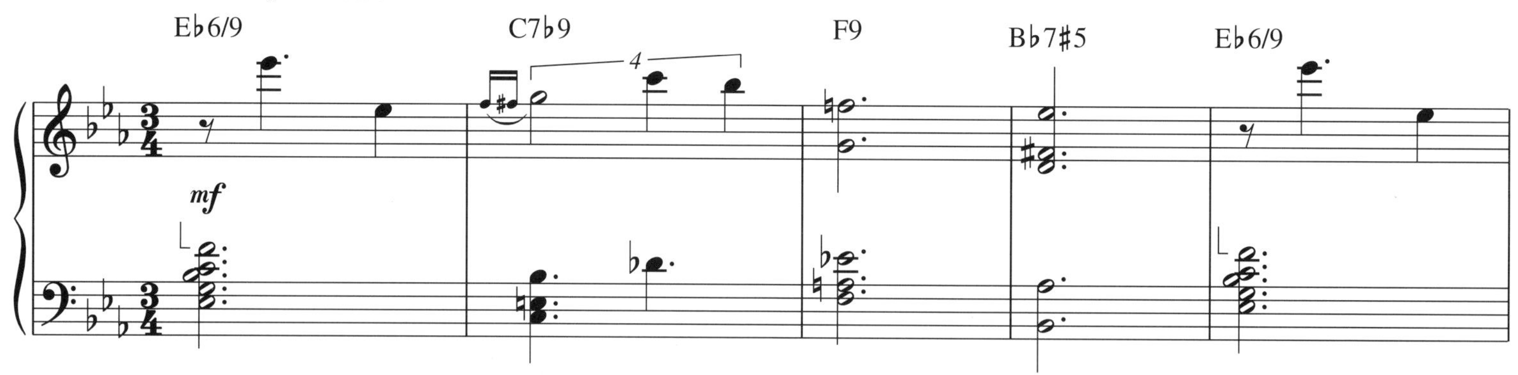

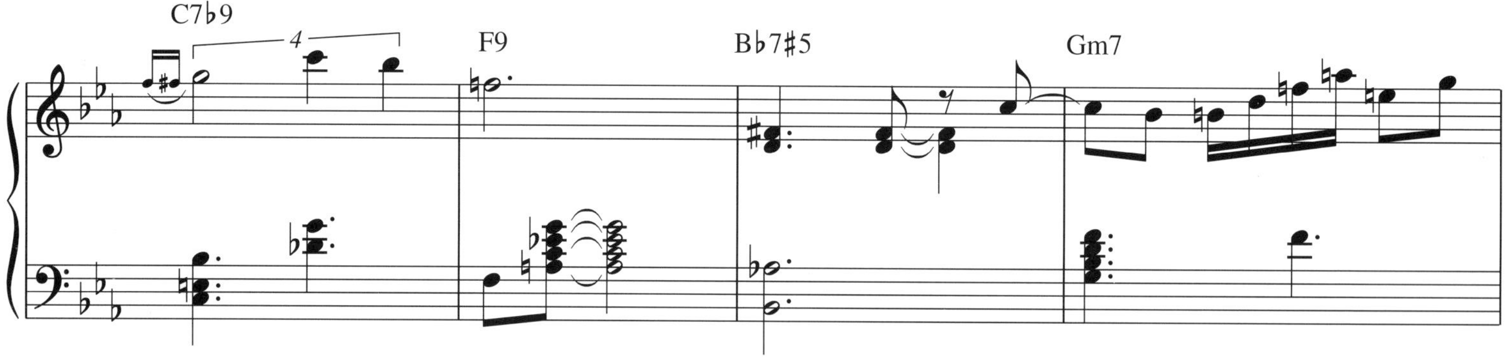

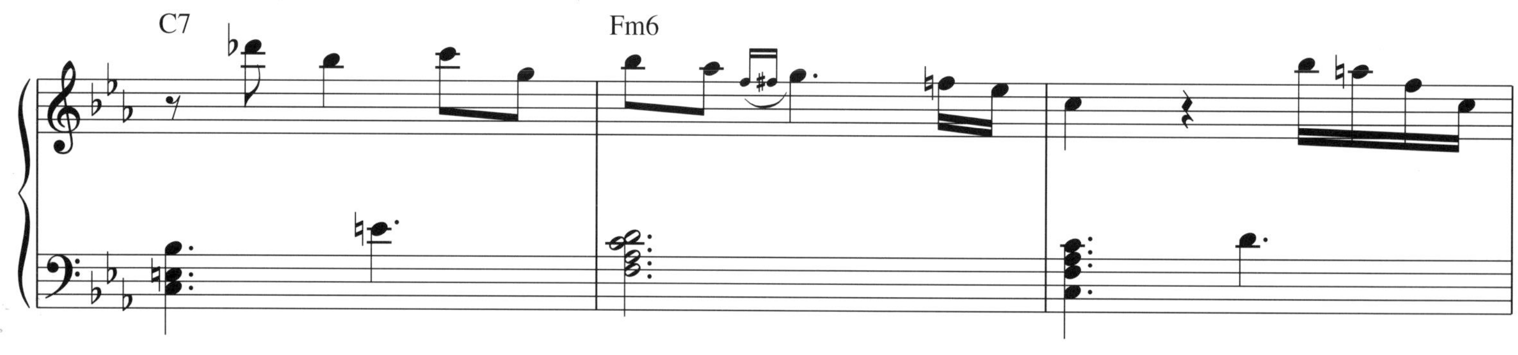

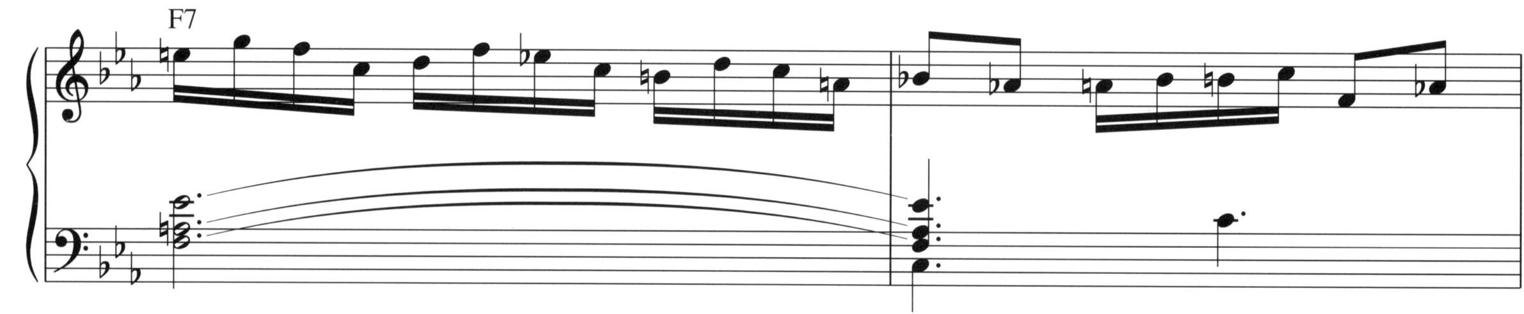

Fm7
Bb13
Bb7#5
Eb6/9
C7b9
4
F9
Bb7#5
Eb9sus
3
Eb7
Abmaj7
F9/A
4
Gm7/Bb
4
C7b9/G
Fm7
Bb9sus
Bb7#5
Eb6/9
Bb7#5
Eb6/9
C7b9
4
F9

B♭7♯5
E♭6/9
C7♭9
4
F9
B♭7♯5
Gm7
C7
Fm6
F13
4
B♭13
B♭7♯5
E♭6/9
E°7
F7
B♭7♯5
E♭9
A♭maj7
4

F9/A
Gm7/B♭
C7♭9/G
Fm7
F♯dim7
Gm7
C7♭9
Fm7
F♯dim7
Gm7
C7♭9
Fm7
B♭13
E♭6/9/G
D♭9/F
Repeat and Fade
E♭6/9
D♭9
E♭6/9
D♭9
Optional Ending
E♭6/9

BLUE CHARLIE BROWN

By VINCE GUARALDI

Medium Jazz Blues

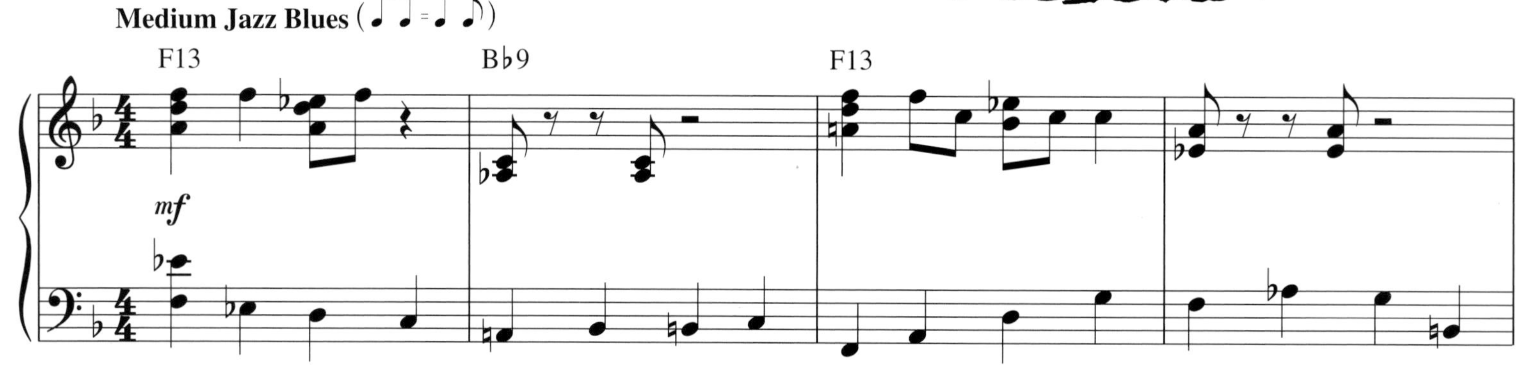

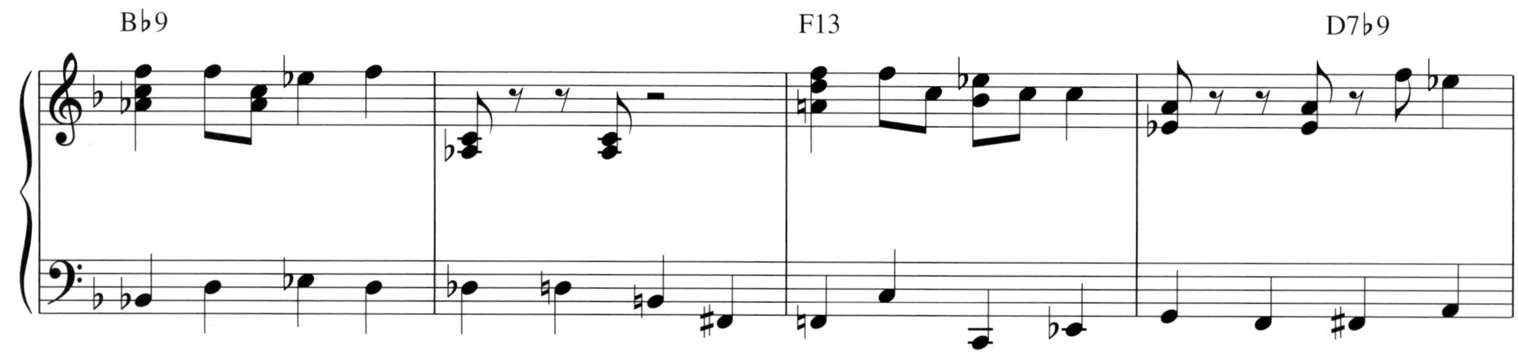

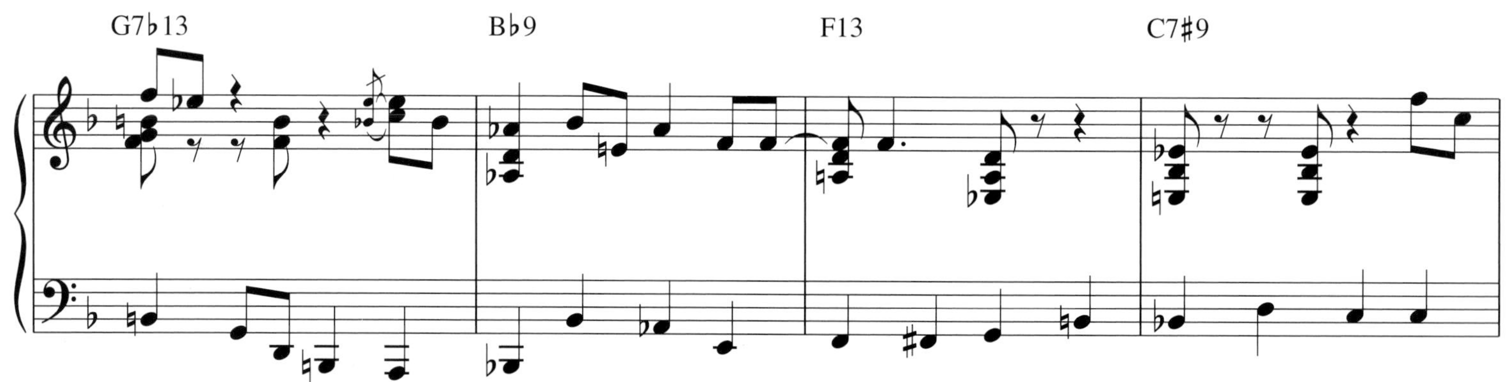

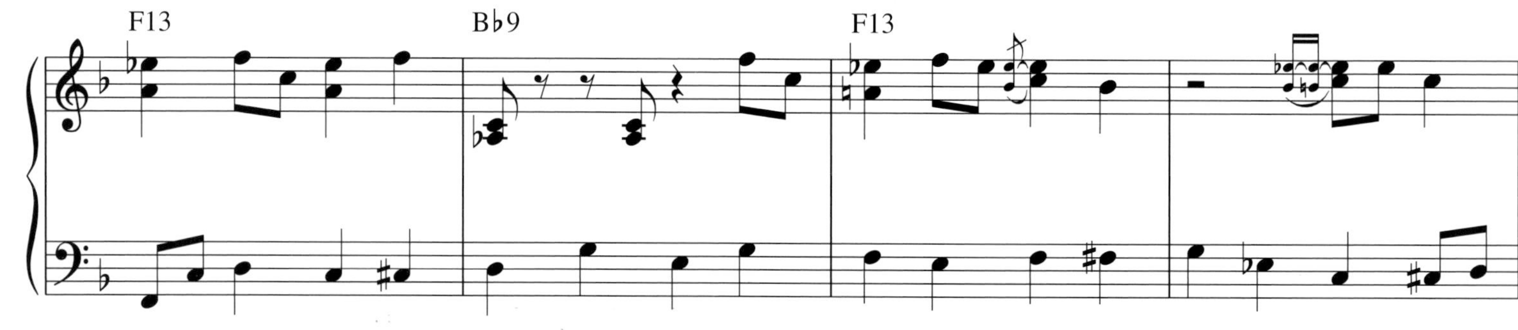

B♭9
F13
D7♭9
Gm7
C7
F13
C7♯9
F13
B♭9
F13
F7♭13
B♭9
F13
D7♭9
Gm7
C7

F13
D7♭9
Gm7
C7
F13
B♭9
F13
B♭9
F13
Gm7
C7
F13
1.
C7#9
2.
C7#9
F13
B♭9
F13
B♭9

F13
D7♭9
Gm7
F13
Gm7
C7
F13
B♭9
F13
B♭9
F13

CAMPTOWN RACES
Traditional
Arranged by VINCE GUARALDI
Quickly
N.C.
Play 4 times
f
Eb6/9
F13
Bb13/F
Bb9
Eb6/9
F13
Bb13
Eb6
Eb6/9
F13
Bb13
Eb6/9

F13
B♭13
E♭
E♭maj7
E♭7
A♭
A♭m
E♭
E♭6/9
F9
B♭7
E♭13
D♭13
To Coda
E♭13
D♭13
Play 3 times
piano solo
E♭13
D♭13
Repeat ad lib.
D.S. al Coda
CODA
E♭13/B♭
D♭13/B♭
Repeat and Fade
Optional Ending
E♭13
D♭13

CHARLIE'S BLUES

By VINCE GUARALDI

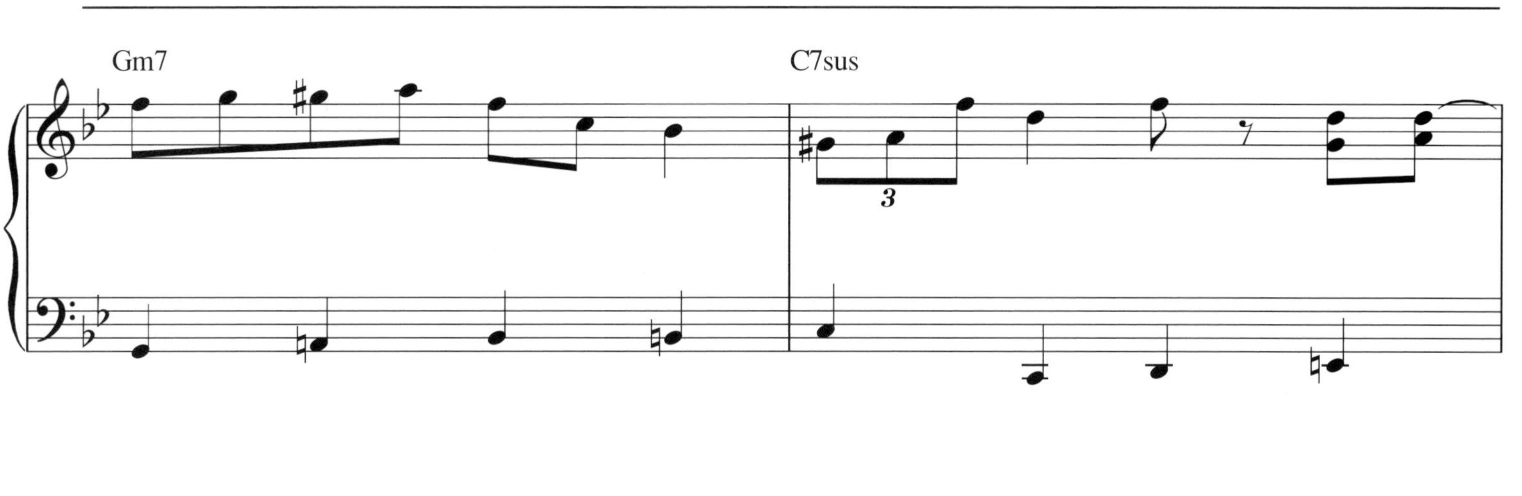
Gm7
C7sus
3

F13
F7♯5
2.
F13

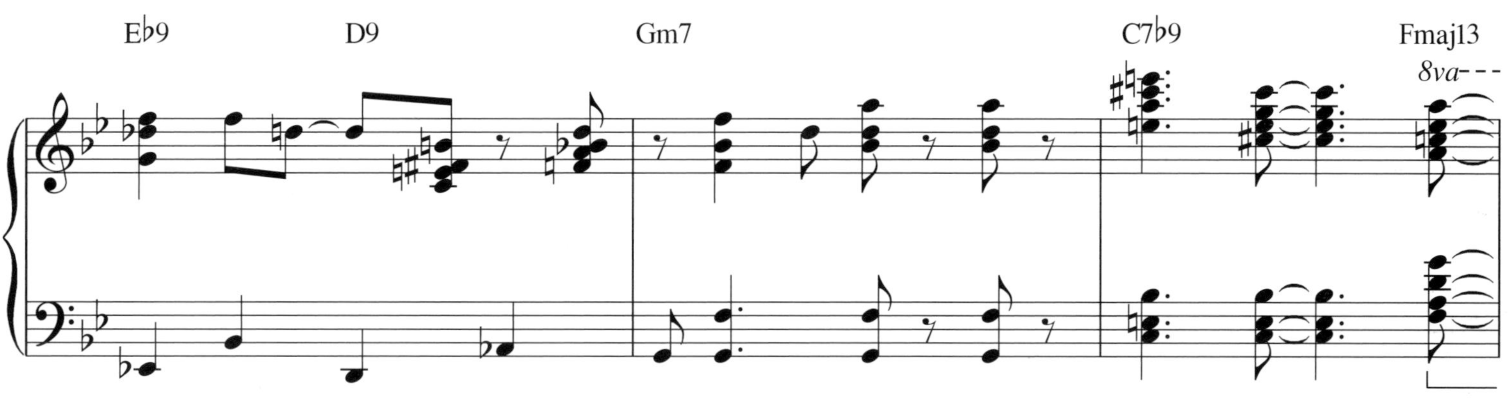
E♭9
D9
Gm7
C7♭9
Fmaj13
8va

CHARLIE BROWN THEME

By VINCE GUARALDI

Medium Swing

G G7 C D7 G G7 C C#dim G/D C#dim G/D C#dim A7 D7 G

mp

G7
C
D7
G
G7
C
C♯dim
G
C♯dim
G/D
C♯dim
A7
D7
To Coda
G
G7
Cmaj7

D7
G
G7
C
Cdim
G/D
Cdim
G/D
C♯dim
A7
D7
G
D.C. al Coda
CODA
G
C♯dim
p-pp
G/D
C♯dim
1.
A7
D7
G
2.
A7
D7
G

CHRISTMAS TIME IS HERE
Words by LEE MENDELSON
Music by VINCE GUARALDI
Slowly
With pedal
Fmaj9 C13♭9 Fmaj9 C13♭9
Fmaj9 E♭13♯11 Fmaj9
Christ - mas time is here, hap - pi - ness and
Snow - flakes in the air, car - ols ev - 'ry -
E♭13♯11 Bm7♭5 B♭m7 Am7 A♭m7
cheer. Fun for all that chil - dren call their
where. Old - en times and an - cient rhymes of
Gm7 Gm7♭5/C 1. Fmaj9 2. Fmaj9
fa - v'rite time of year.
love and dreams to share.

Dbmaj7
Gb13#11
Dbmaj7
Gb13#11
Sleigh-bells in the air, beau-ty ev-'ry-where.
Am7
Eb9
D9
D7b9
Gm7
Db9
C13
C13b9
Yule-tide by the fire-side and joy-ful mem-'ries there.
Fmaj9
Eb13#11
Fmaj9
E13#11
Christ-mas time is here, we'll be draw-ing near.
To Coda
Bm7b5
Bbm7
Am7
Abm7
Gm7
Bb/C
Fmaj9
Oh, that we could al-ways see such spir-it through the year.

Eb13#11
Fmaj9
Eb13#11
Bm7b5
Bbm7

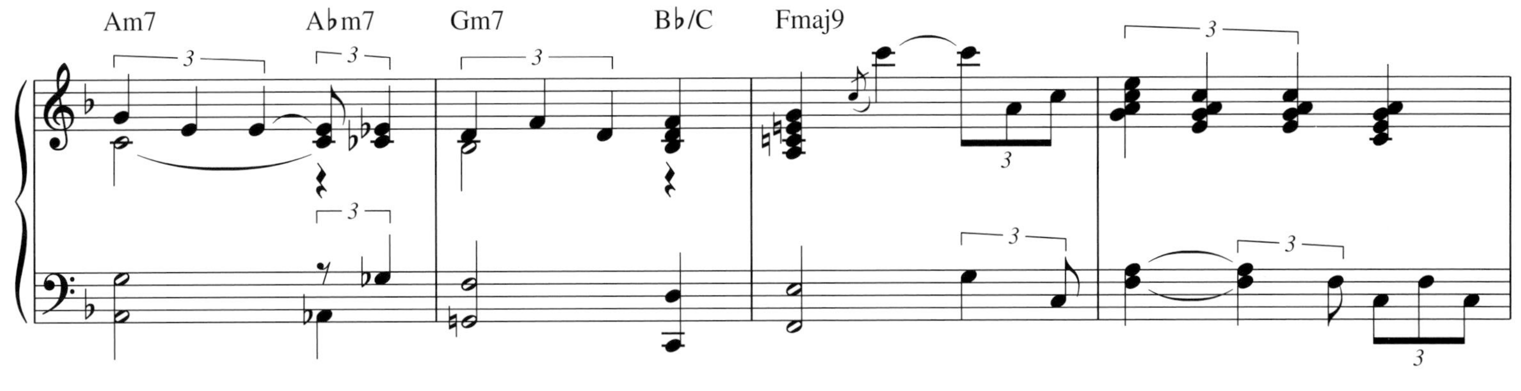
Am7
Abm7
Gm7
Bb/C
Fmaj9

Eb13#11
Fmaj9
Eb13#11
Bm7b5
Bbm7
Am7
Abm7

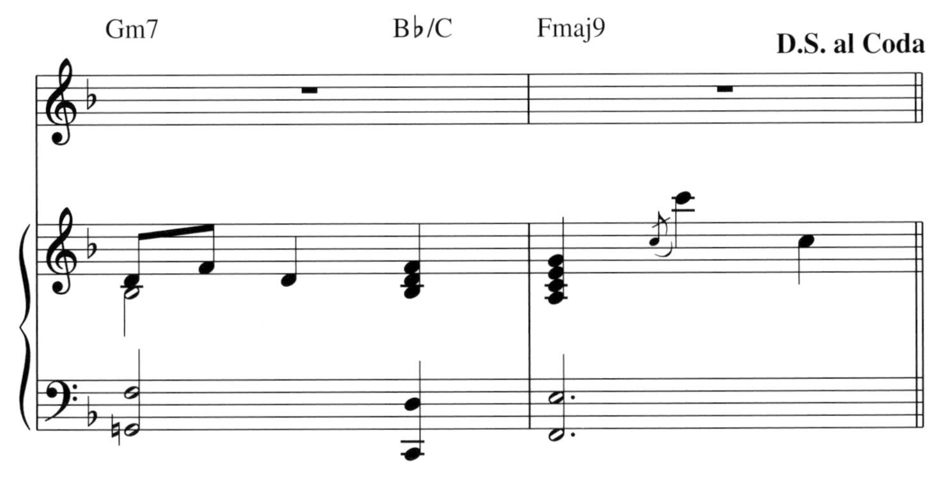
Gm7
Bb/C
Fmaj9
D.S. al Coda

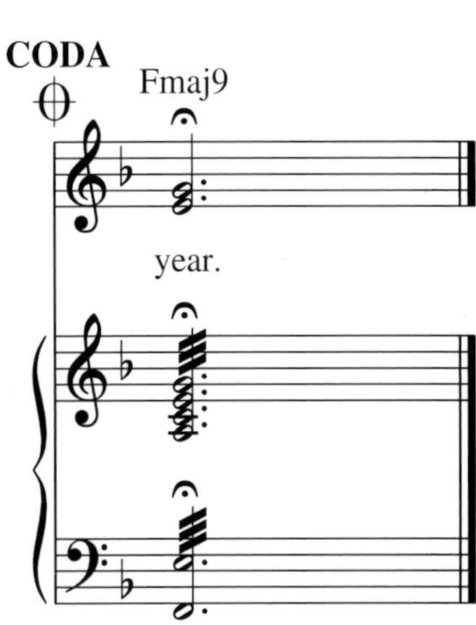
CODA
Fmaj9
year.

CHRISTMAS IS COMING
By VINCE GUARALDI
Bright Bossa, Rock feel
N.C.
Ab/Bb
f
With pedal
Eb/Bb
Ab/Bb
Eb/Bb
Ab/Bb
Am7b5
Abm6
Eb/G
Gbdim7
Fm7
Fm7/Bb
Eb6/9/Bb
Ab
Eb/Bb
Ab/Bb
Eb/Bb
Ab/Bb

Am7♭5
A♭m6
E♭/G
G♭dim7
Fm7
Fm7/B♭
E♭6/9
C
A♭7
mp
N.C.
A♭
f
E♭/B♭
A♭/B♭
3

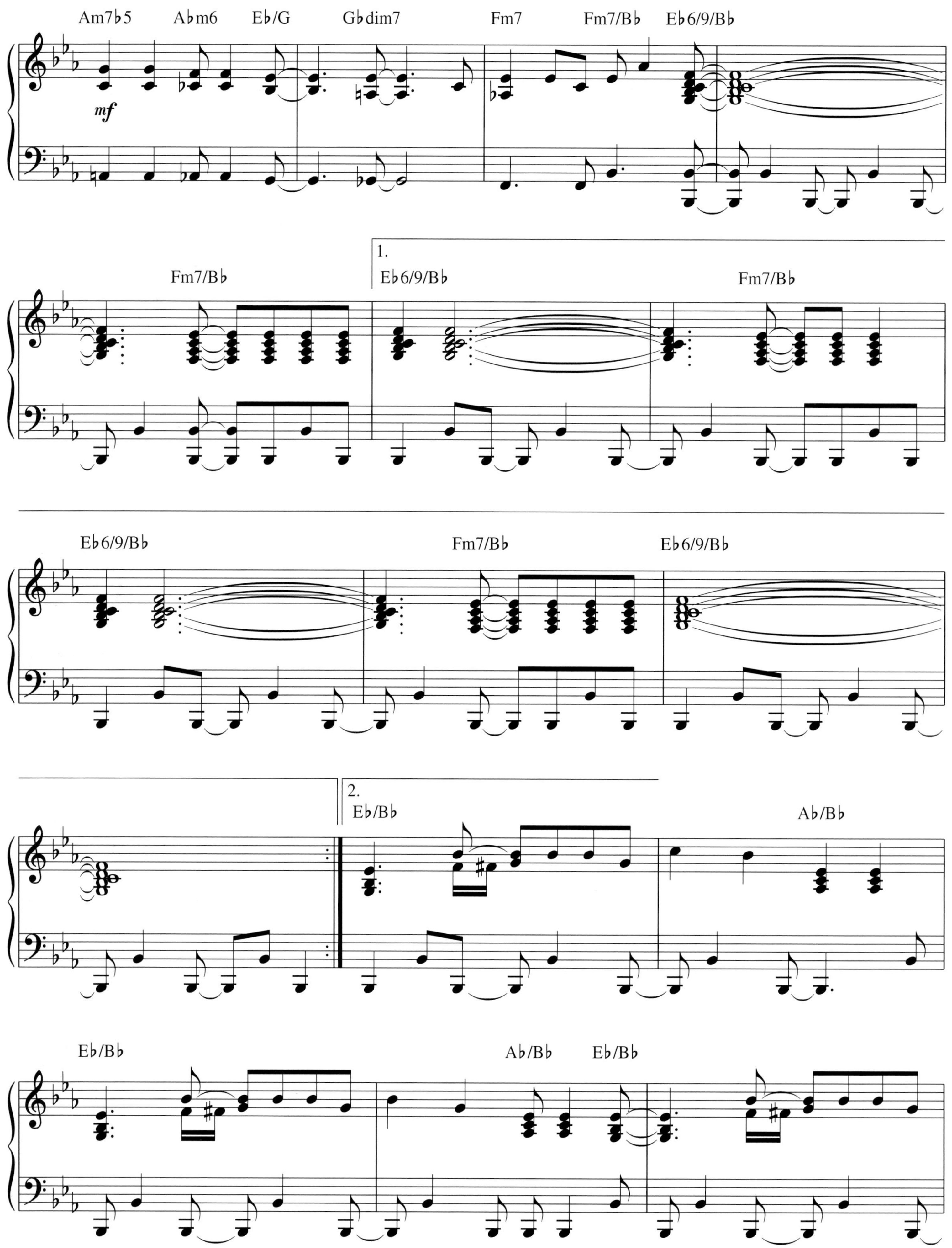
Am7♭5
A♭m6
E♭/G
G♭dim7
Fm7
Fm7/B♭
E♭6/9/B♭
mf
Fm7/B♭
1.
E♭6/9/B♭
Fm7/B♭
E♭6/9/B♭
Fm7/B♭
E♭6/9/B♭
2.
E♭/B♭
A♭/B♭
E♭/B♭
A♭/B♭
E♭/B♭

Ab/Bb
Eb/Bb
Ab/Bb
Eb/Bb
Ab/Bb
Eb/Bb
Ab/Bb
Eb/Bb
Ab/Bb
Eb/Bb
Ab/Bb
Eb/Bb
Ab/Bb
Eb/Bb
Ab/Bb
Eb/Bb
Ab/Bb
Eb/Bb
Ab/Bb
Eb/Bb
Ab/Bb
dim.
Eb/Bb
Ab/Bb
Eb/Bb
Ab/Bb
Eb/Bb
Ab/Bb
Eb/Bb
Ab/Bb
Eb6/9
mp
f
8vb

THE CHRISTMAS SONG (CHESTNUTS ROASTING ON AN OPEN FIRE)

Music and Lyric by MEL TORME
and ROBERT WELLS

F
Em7♭5
A7
Dm
Dm/C
Bm7♭5
B♭m6
Fmaj7/A
C7/G
B♭m6
rit.
Am
Bm11
E7♭9/B
Am7
D7♭9
Gm7
D♭7
C7
F(add2)
rit.
Cm7
F13
F7
Dm7
G7♭13
G7
Cm7
F13
F7♭13
B♭maj9
B♭m7
E♭7
A♭6/9
dim.
G7♭13
mp
dim.
C7♯9
C7♭9(♭13)
p
cresc.
F
B♭
mf

Am Gm F C13♭9 F Em7♭5 A7 Dm Dm/C Bm7♭5 B♭m6
Fmaj7/A C7/G B♭m6 Am Bm7♭5 E7♭9/B Am D7♯9 Gm7 C7♭9 F6/9
rit.
Slowly
Cm7 F13 Dm7 G7♭13
Cm7 F13 F7♭13 B♭maj9
B♭m7 E♭7sus E♭7

Abmaj7
Ab6/9
Ab7
G7#9(b13)
Gm9/C
C13b9
C7b9(b13)
F
Bb
Am7
Gm7
Fmaj7
C13b9
F6/9
Em7b5
A7b9
Dm
Dm/C
G7/B
Bbm
F/A
C7/G
Bbm6
Am
Bm7b5
E7
Am7
D7b9
Gm7
C7b9
Am7
Eb7
D7
Gm9
Bb/C
C7b9
rit.
Rubato
Bm7b5
Bbmaj7
Am7
Abdim7
Gm7
Gm7b5/C
Fmaj13#11
accel.
rit.

FRIEDA (WITH THE NATURALLY CURLY HAIR)

By VINCE GUARALDI

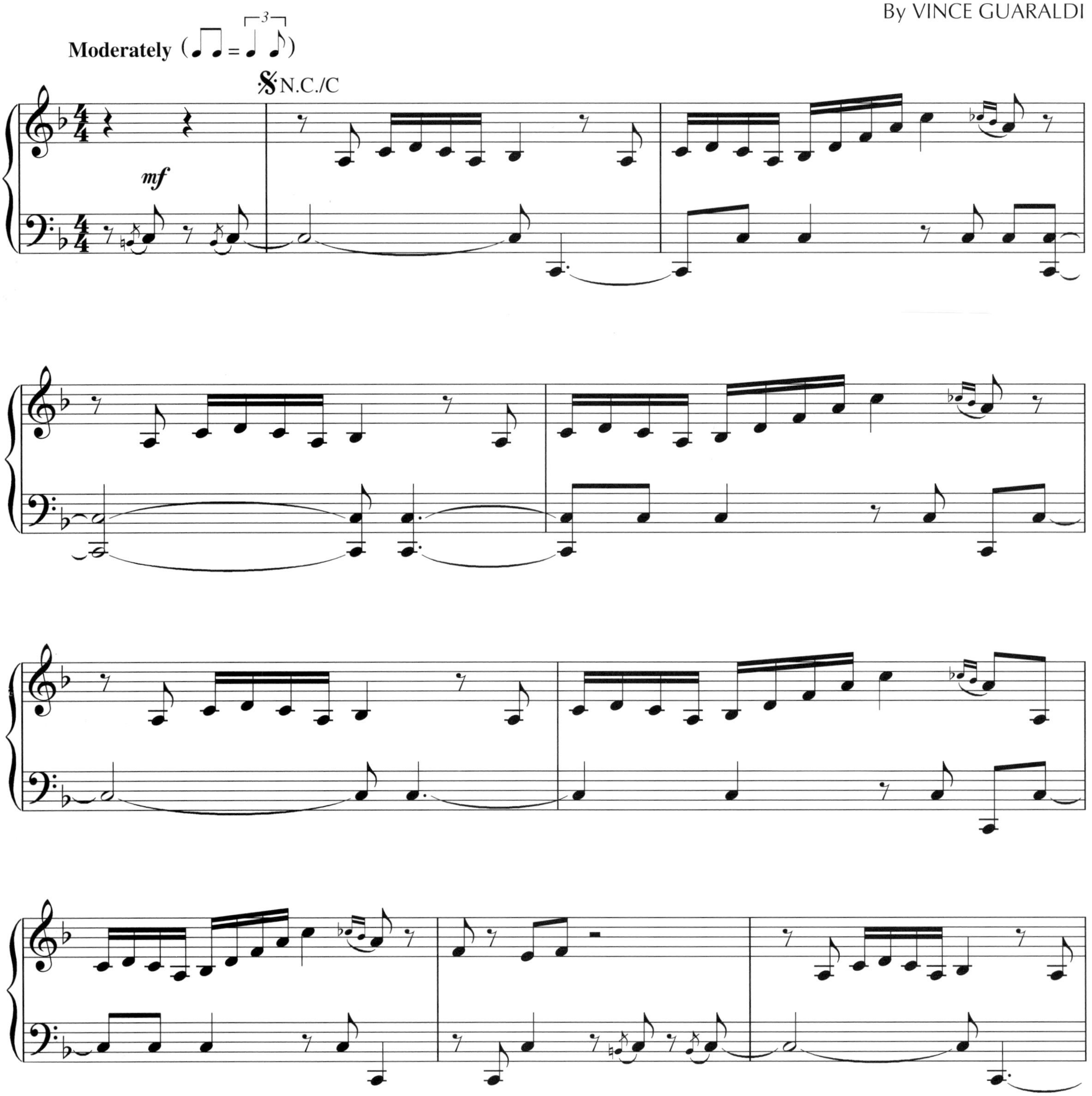

Moderately

N.C./C

mf

F
A7sus
A7
D7
G7
3

D7♯9
Gm7
C7♭9
N.C./C
To Coda
F
C pedal
F
D7
Gm7
C7

F
D7
Gm7
F7
B♭7
G7
F
D7
Gm7
C7
F
D7
Gm7
C7
Am7
D7
G7
C7
F7
3
B♭7
Bdim
F/C
D7sus
C7
F

A7
D7
3
G7
3
Gm7
3
C7sus
F
D7
G7
3
C7
A
3
D7
G7
3
C7
F
D7

1. Repeat ad lib. 2.

B♭7 Bdim F/C D7 Gm7 C7sus Gm7 C7sus

D.S. al Coda

CODA

F N.C./C

Repeat and Fade

Optional Ending

N.C.

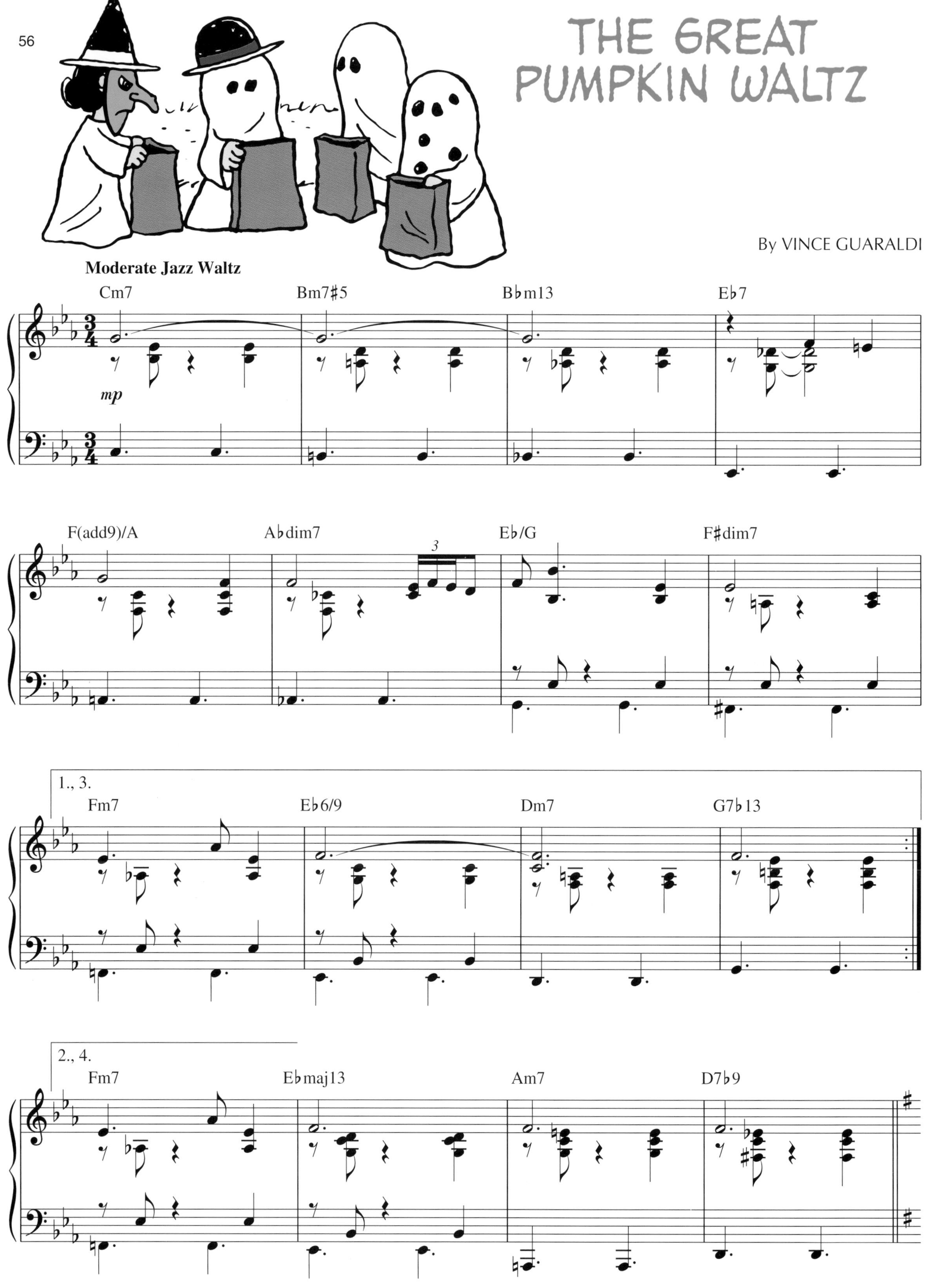
THE GREAT PUMPKIN WALTZ
By VINCE GUARALDI
Moderate Jazz Waltz
Cm7
Bm7♯5
B♭m13
E♭7
mp
F(add9)/A
A♭dim7
3
E♭/G
F♯dim7
1., 3.
Fm7
E♭6/9
Dm7
G7♭13
2., 4.
Fm7
E♭maj13
Am7
D7♭9

G(add9)
Cm(maj7)
Cm6
G
Cm(maj7)
G(add9)
Cm(maj7)
Cm6
G
G♭+
F6
G7♯5
Cm7
Bm7♯5
B♭m13

E♭7
F(add9)/A
A♭dim7
3
E♭/G
F♯dim7
Fm7
To Coda
E♭6/9
Dm7
G7♭9
D.C. al Coda
CODA
Fm7
E♭6/9
Repeat and Fade
Optional Ending

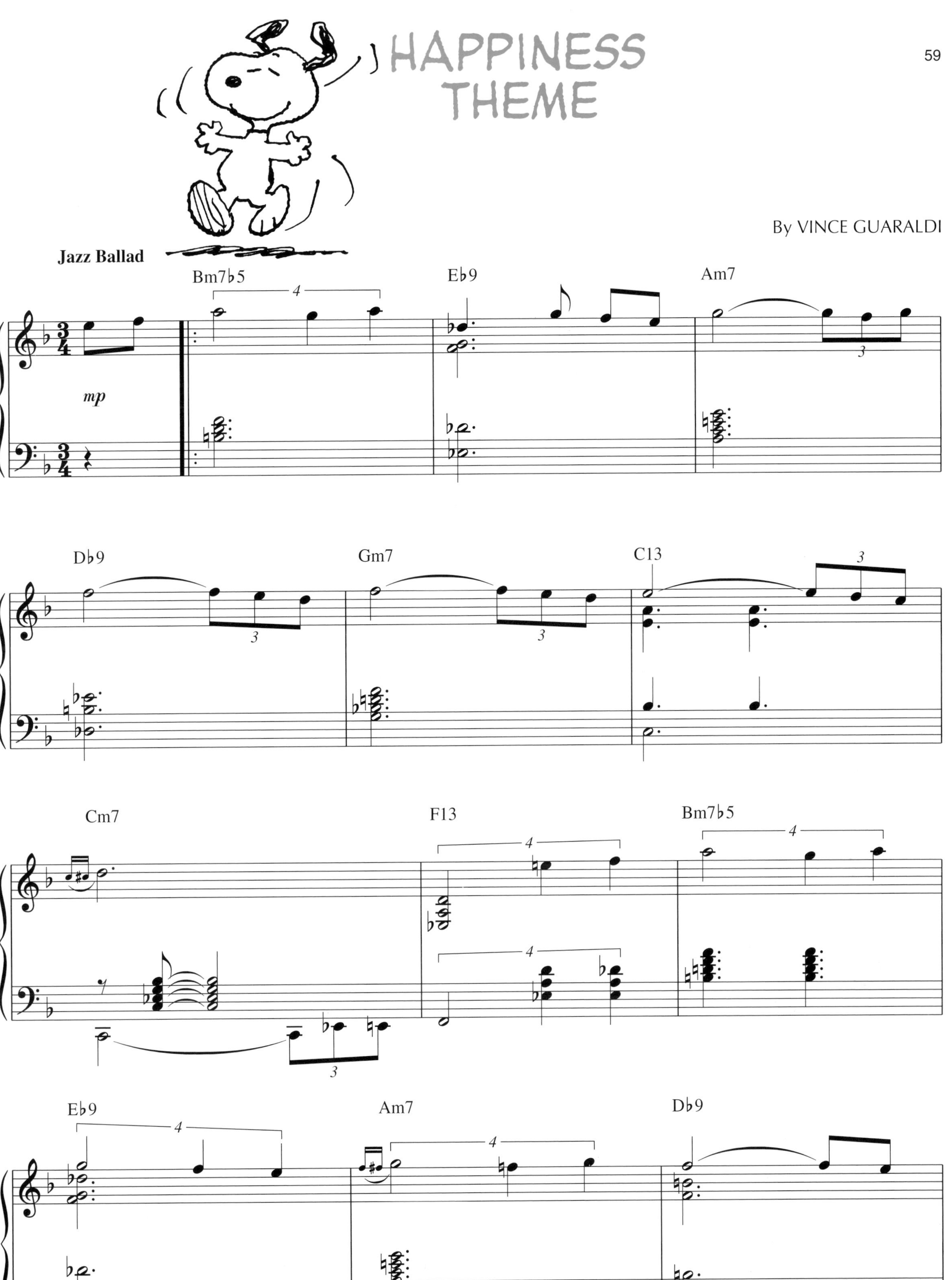
HAPPINESS THEME
By VINCE GUARALDI
Jazz Ballad
mp
Bm7♭5
E♭9
Am7
D♭9
Gm7
C13
Cm7
F13
Bm7♭5
E♭9
Am7
D♭9

Gm7
C13
Fmaj9
Em7
A7#5
A7
Dm7
Dm7/D♭
Dm7/C
G13
G7♭13
Gm7
C13
C7♭13
Bm7♭5
E♭9
Am7
D♭9
Gm7
1.
C13
Fmaj9
D7#5(♭9)

2.
C13
Fmaj9
Eb6/9
Fmaj9
Eb6/9
Fmaj9
Eb6/9
Fmaj9
Eb6/9
Fmaj9
Eb6/9
Fmaj9
Eb6/9
F6/9

HARK, THE HERALD ANGELS SING

Traditional
Arranged by VINCE GUARALDI

C7/E F F/C C F/A C7/E F F/C C
na - tions rise; join the tri - umph of the skies;
B♭ D Gm C C7/B♭ F/A F/C C F
with an - gel - ic hosts pro - claim, "Christ is born in Beth - le - hem!"
B♭ D Gm C/E C7/B♭ F/A F/C C F
Hark! The her - ald an - gels sing, "Glo - ry to the new - born King!"

HE'S YOUR DOG, CHARLIE BROWN

By VINCE GUARALDI

Moderately fast

Ab Db Eb

mf

Db Ab Db

Eb Db Eb

Db Eb Db

E♭
D♭
N.C.
A♭
D♭
E♭
D♭
Cm
B♭m
A♭
N.C.
A♭
D♭
1.
E♭
D♭
Cm
B♭m
A♭
Repeat ad lib.
2.
E♭
D♭
Cm
B♭m
Repeat ad lib. and Fade
E♭
D♭
Cm
B♭m
Optional Ending
E♭
D♭
Cm
B♭m
A♭

HEARTBURN WALTZ

By VINCE GUARALDI

Moderate Jazz Waltz

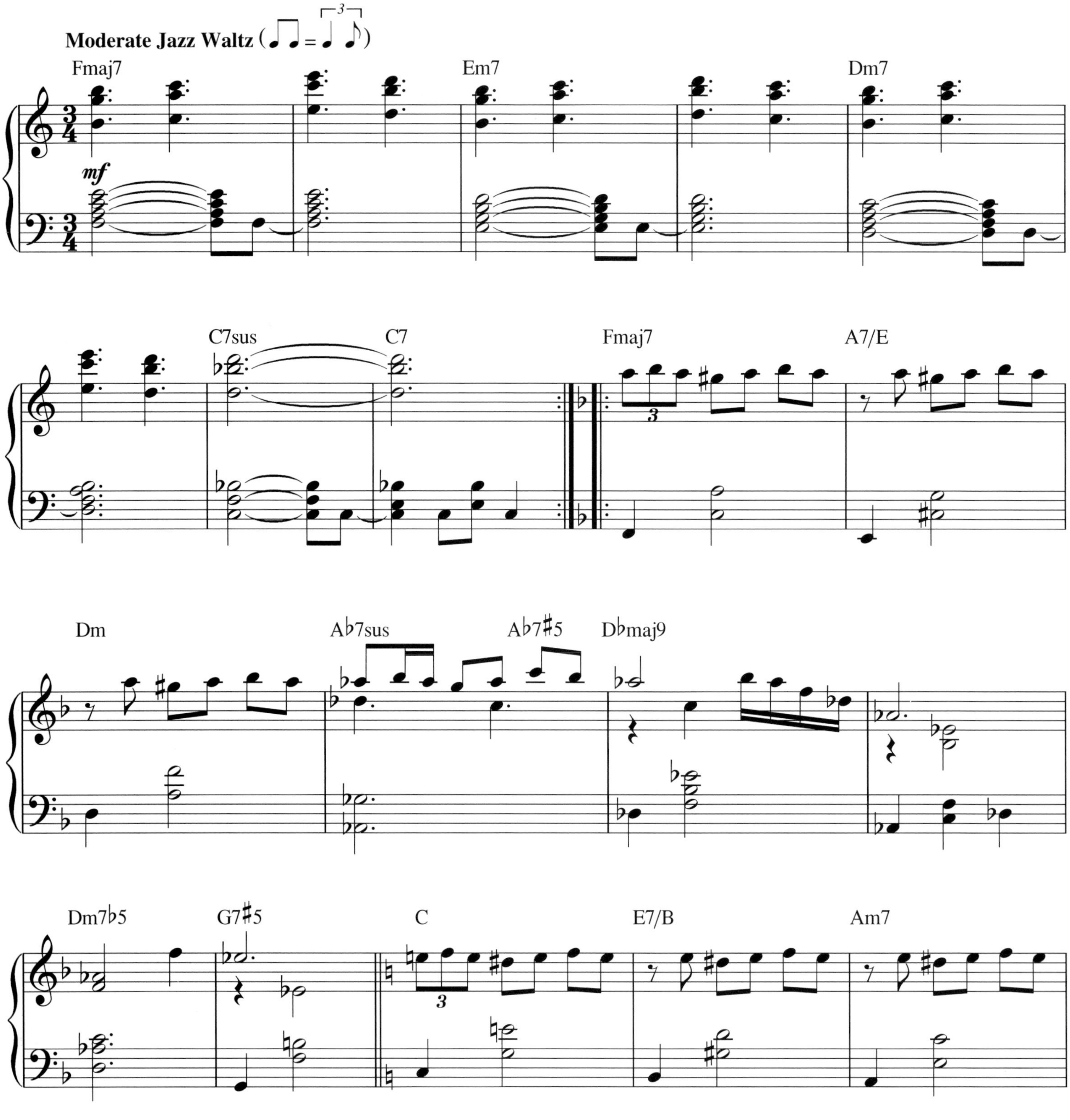

Fmaj7 Em7 Dm7 C7sus C7 Fmaj7 A7/E Dm A♭7sus A♭7♯5 D♭maj9 Dm7♭5 G7♯5 C E7/B Am7

Gm6
Fmaj7
Em7
Dm7
G7
C7sus
1.
C7
2.
C7
Fmaj7
Em7
3
Dm7
G9
1.
C7sus
C7
2.
Cmaj7
G7♯5
Cmaj7
G7♯5
Cmaj7
G7♯5
Cmaj7

JOE COOL

By VINCE GUARALDI

Moderate Swing

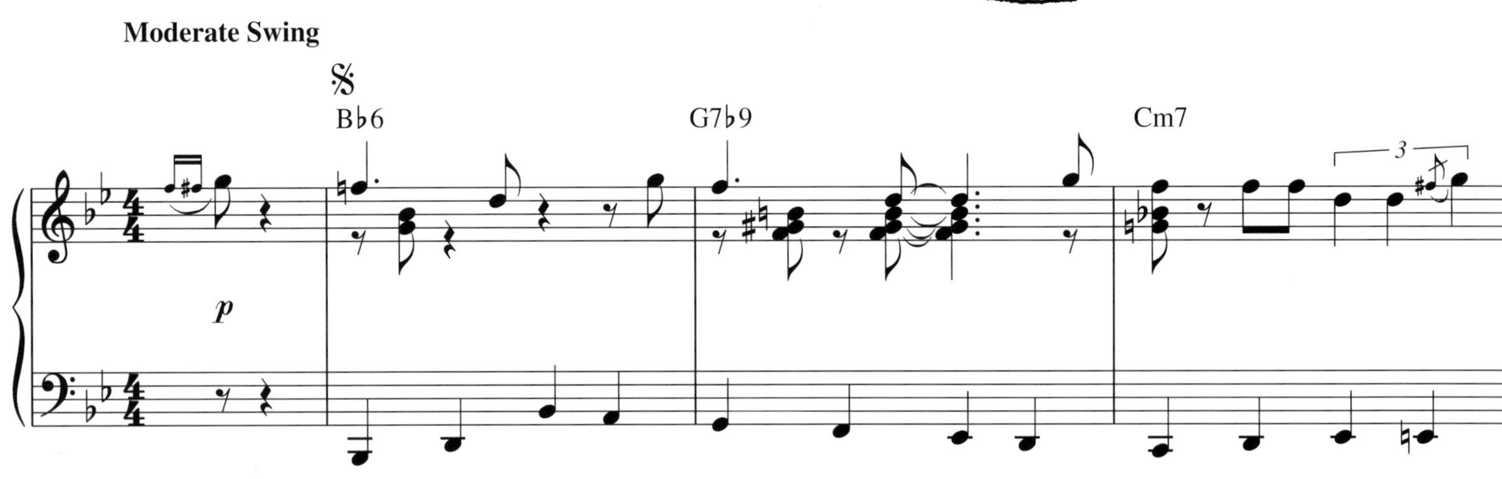

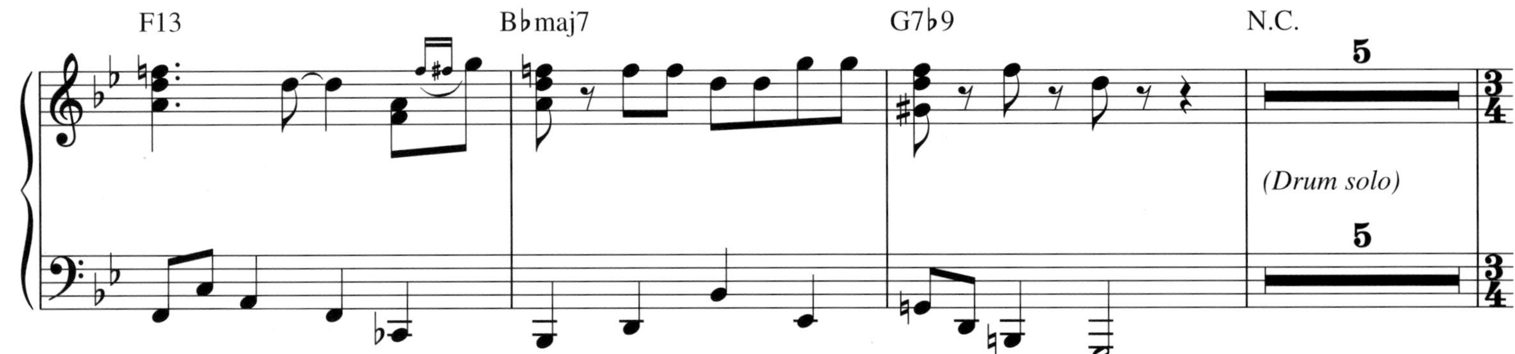

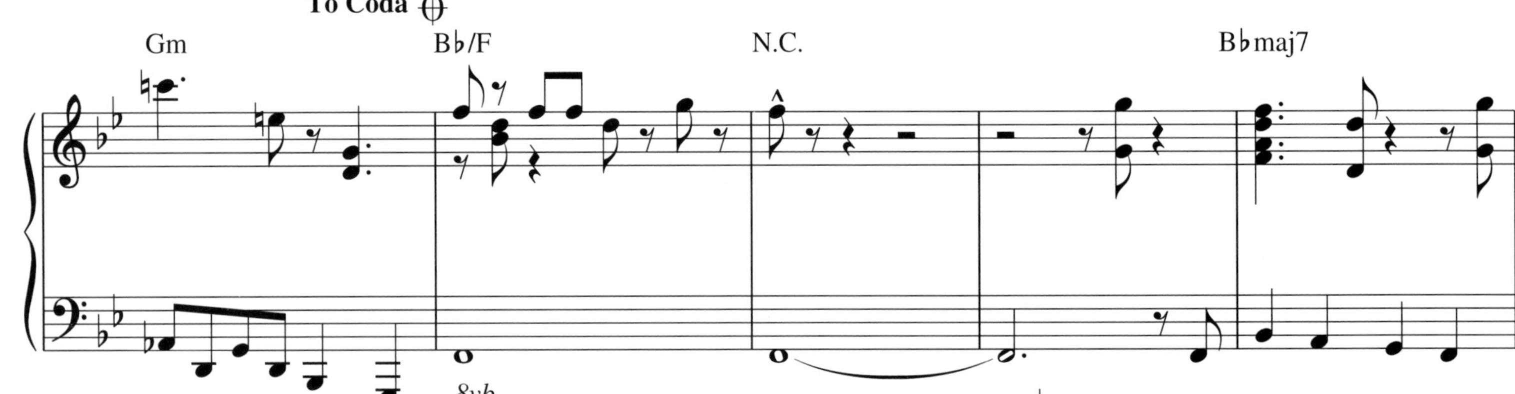

G7♭9
N.C.
E♭maj7
(Drum solo)
A♭9
B♭maj7
Gm
B♭/F
8vb
Bdim7/F
F7(sus2)
Adim7/B♭ B♭(add9)
March tempo
E♭/B♭
(8vb)
C/B♭
Fm/B♭
B♭7
N.C.
tr
D.S. al Coda
CODA
B♭maj7/F
Bdim/F
F7(sus2)
Adim7/B♭ B♭(add9)
8vb

LINUS AND LUCY

By VINCE GUARALDI

D♭
E♭sus
N.C.
D♭
E♭sus
N.C.
D♭
E♭sus
N.C.
A♭
A♭
C♭
A♭
C♭
A♭

Swing (♫ = ♩♪)
N.C.
E9
Eb9
To Coda
Db9
C9
Db9
Eb9
E9
Eb9
Db9
C9

D.S. al Coda
D♭9
D9
E♭9
A♭
CODA
N.C.
A♭

LOVE WILL COME

By VINCE GUARALDI

Moderately, expressively

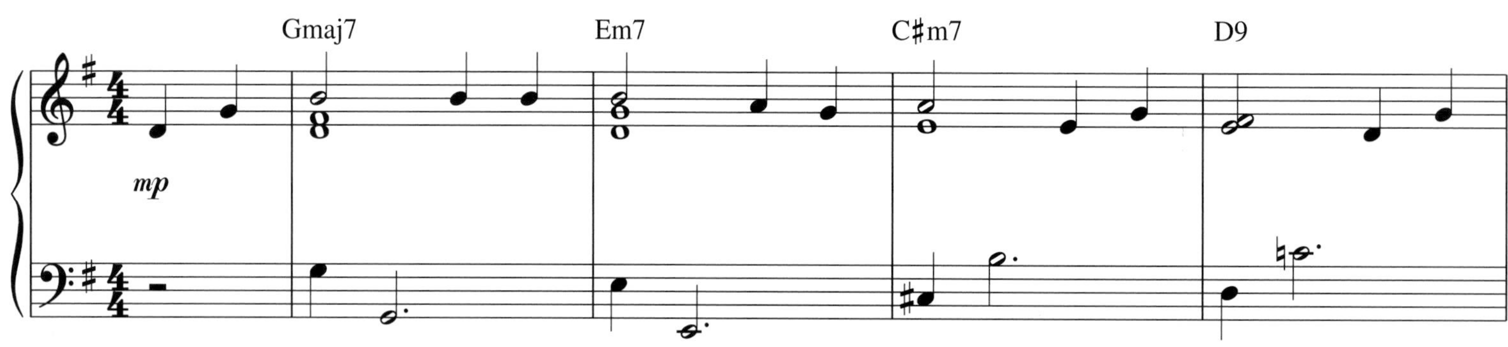

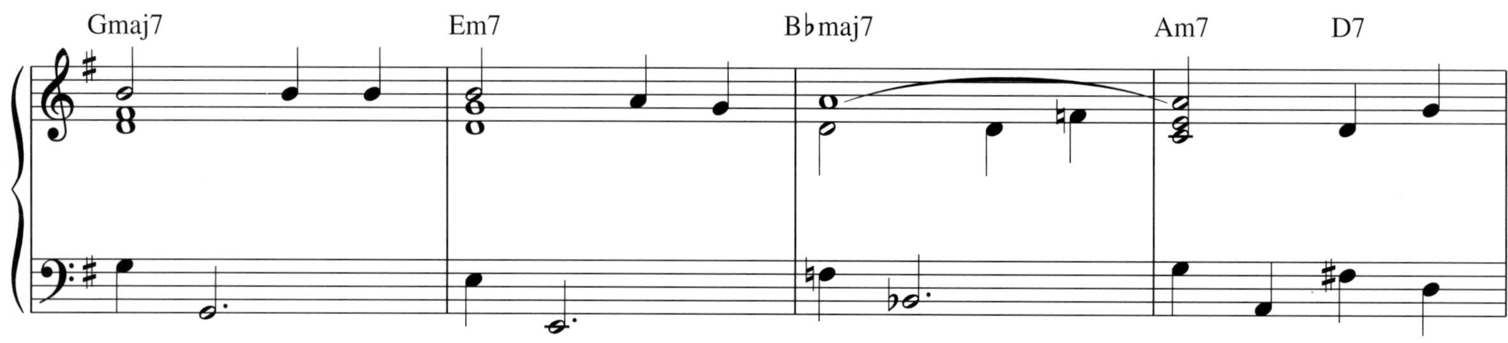

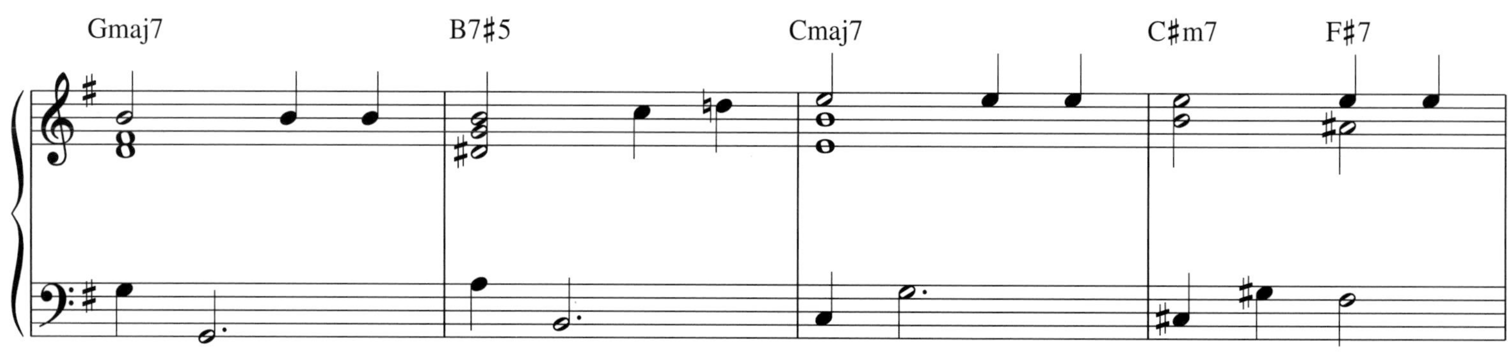

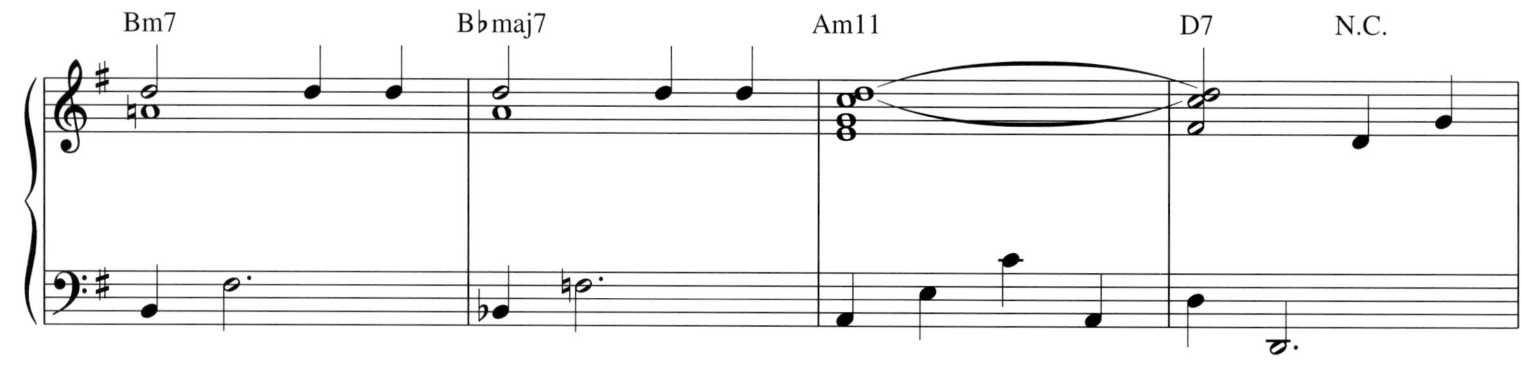

Gmaj7
Em7
C♯m7
D9
Gmaj7
Em7
B♭maj7
Am7
D7
Gmaj7
B7♯5
Cmaj7
C♯m7
F♯7
Bm7
B♭maj7
Am7
Dm7/G
G13♭9
C♯m7♭5
Cm7
Bm7
E♭7/B♭
Am7
Gmaj9
Fmaj7
Gmaj9

MY LITTLE DRUM

By VINCE GUARALDI

2.,4.
N.C./B♭
N.C./F
To Coda
Fmaj9
F9
(ostinato ends)
Ooh

Bm7♭5
B♭m6
F(add2)/A
A♭dim7
Gm7
Gm7/C
Fmaj9
Gm7/C
Fmaj9
F7
Ooh
Bm7♭5
B♭m6
F(add2)/A
A♭dim7
Gm7
C9
Fmaj9

Eb/F
F7sus
F7
Bbmaj7
Bb7
Ooh
Em7b5
Ebm6
Bb/D
Dbdim7
Cm7
F7
F7/Bb
Bb6
Bbmaj7
Bb6
Fmaj9
F9
Ooh

Bm7♭5
B♭m6
F/A
A♭m7
Gm7
B♭m/C
Fmaj9
D.S. al Coda
3
3
3
CODA
N.C./F
Repeat and Fade
Optional Ending

O TANNENBAUM
Traditional
Arranged by VINCE GUARALDI
Freely
C7♭9 F Gm7 Am F♯dim7 Gm Em7♭5 F B♭m/C
mp
With pedal
F Gm7 Am7 E♭9♯11 D7♭9 Gm C9 F
Am7 D7♭9 Gm7 C13 C7♭13 Fmaj9 C13♭9
F Gm7 Am7 E♭9♯11 D9 Gm7 C7♭9 F6/9 C13♭9
mf

Moderate Swing
F6/9
Gm7
Am7
D7♭9
Gm7
C7♭9
F
Gm7
A7♭13
D7♭9
Gm7
C7♭9
F
Fmaj9
D7♯9/F♯
Gm7
C7♭9
Am7
Dm7
Gm7
C7
Fmaj7
Gm7
Am7♭5
D7♭9
Gm7
C7
1.
F
2.
F
C13♭9
F
Gm7
A7♭13
D7♭9

Gm7
C7♭9
F
C13♭9
F
B♭m6/9
A7♭13
D7♭9
Gm7
C7♭9
F
Fmaj9
D7♯9/F♯
Gm7
G7♯9
C9
Fmaj9
F
Gm7
Am7♭5
E♭9♯11
D7
A♭7♯11
Gm7
B♭/C
F6/9
F6
Gm7
Gm7/C
F6/9
Gm7
Gm7/C
Freely
F6/9(♯11)
8va
dim.

OH, GOOD GRIEF

By VINCE GUARALDI

Dm7
G13
Dm7
G13
Dm7
G13
Cmaj9
G7♭13
Cmaj9
D9
Dm7
G13
Dm7
G13
Em7
E♭m7
Dm7
G13
G7♭13
Cmaj9

D9
Dm7
G13
Dm7
G13
Dm7
G13
G7♭13
Cmaj9
Dm9
Cmaj9
Dm7
Cmaj9
Dm9
Cmaj9
Dm7
Repeat and Fade
Cmaj9
Optional Ending
Cmaj9

THE PEBBLE BEACH THEME

By VINCE GUARALDI

Moderately, with a Latin feel

F, Bb7#11, Bb7

mf

Fmaj9, Eb9

D7, Gm, Em7b5, A7b9

3
3
D♭9
C9
C7♭9

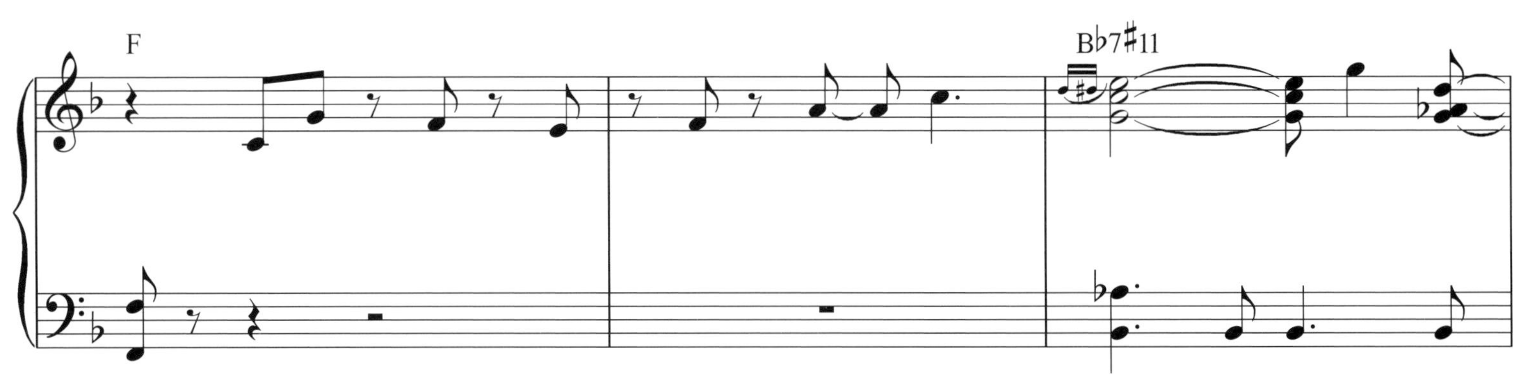
F
B♭7♯11

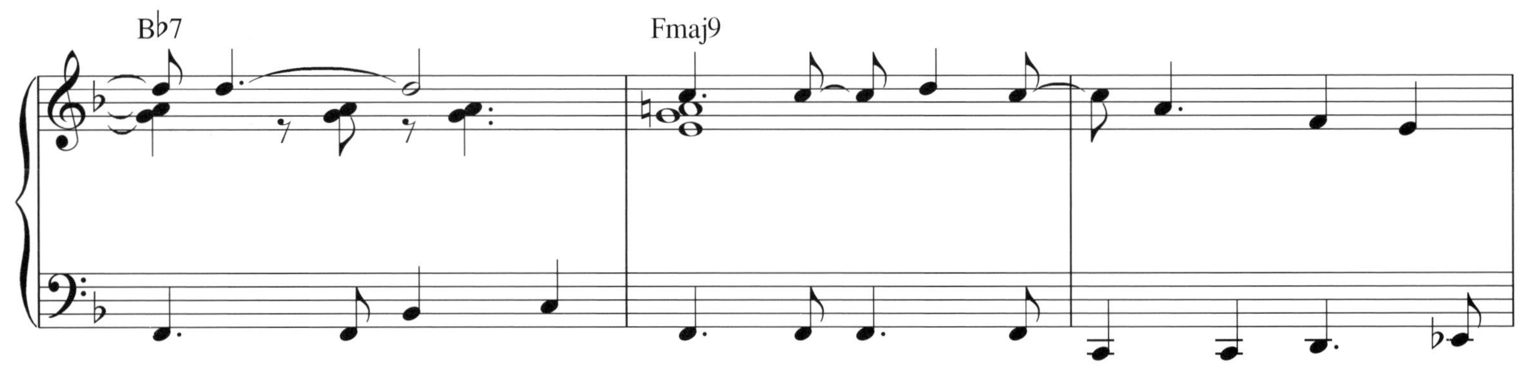
B♭7
Fmaj9

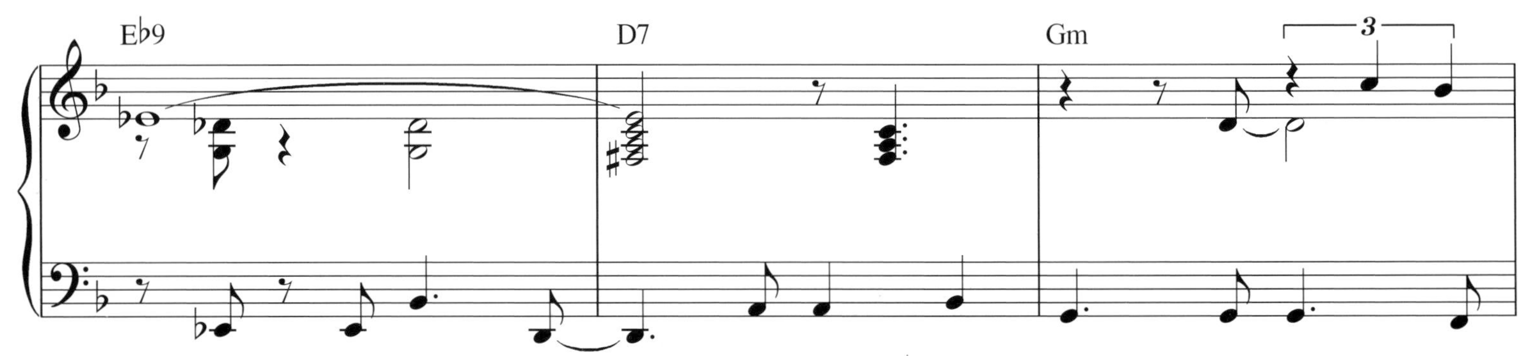
E♭9
D7
Gm
3

Em7♭5
A7♭9
Dm
Bm7♭5
C7
3

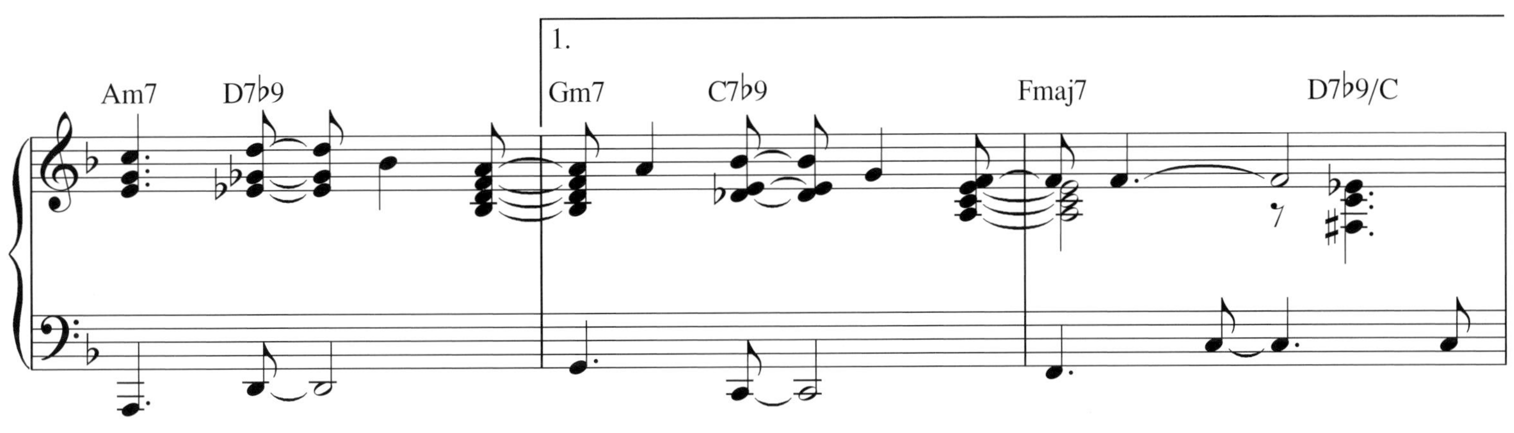
1.
Am7
D7♭9
Gm7
C7♭9
Fmaj7
D7♭9/C

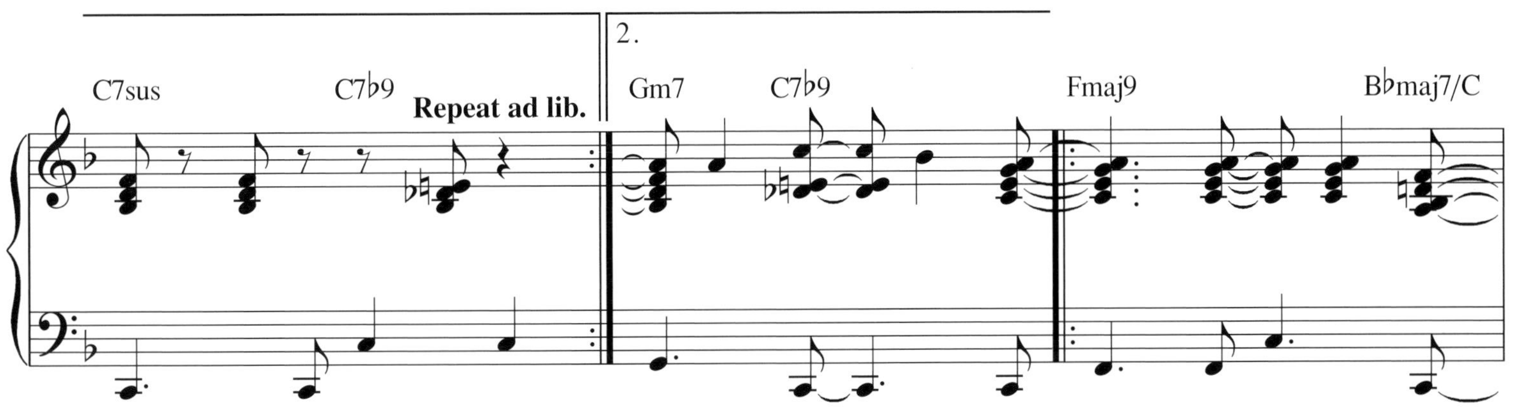
C7sus
C7♭9
Repeat ad lib.
2.
Gm7
C7♭9
Fmaj9
B♭maj7/C

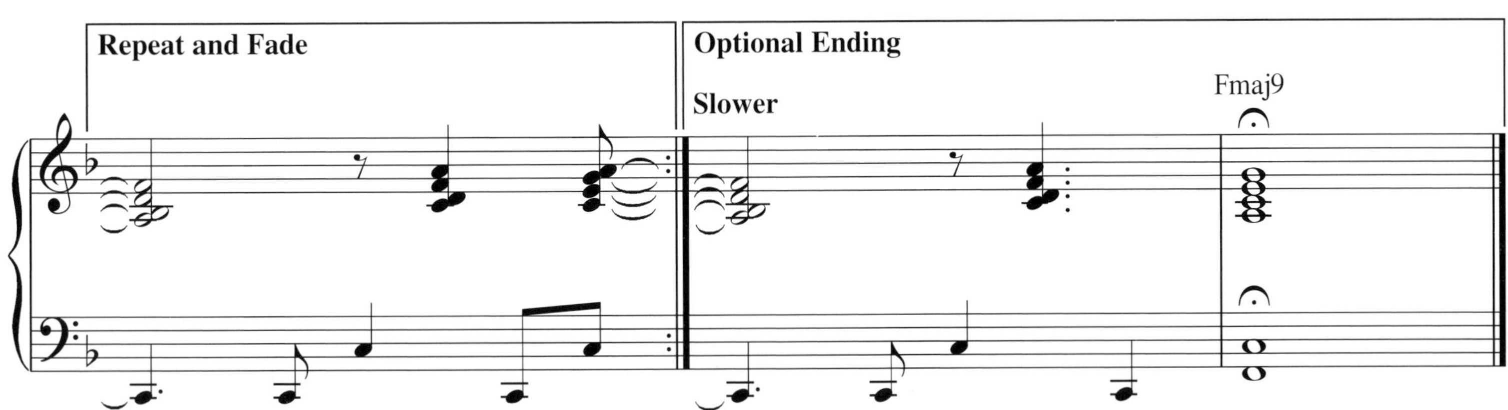
Repeat and Fade
Optional Ending
Slower
Fmaj9

PEPPERMINT PATTY

By VINCE GUARALDI

F
Cm/F
B♭maj9
D♭maj7
E♭6
E♭m7♭5
D.S. al Coda
CODA
N.C.
Play 4 times
F
A♭
E♭
E
Repeat ad lib.
F
A♭
Repeat and Fade
Optional Ending
E♭
E
F
A♭
E♭
E
F

RAIN, RAIN, GO AWAY

By VINCE GUARALDI

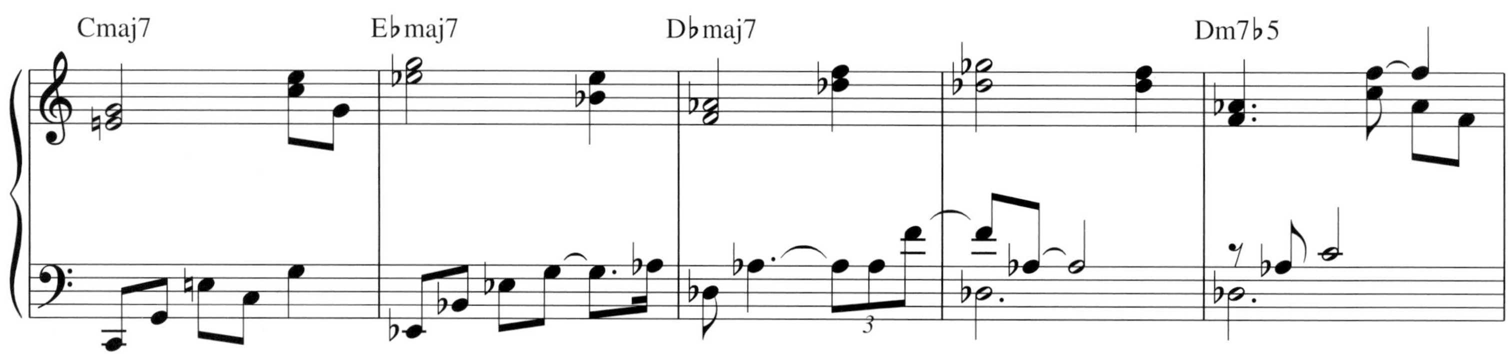

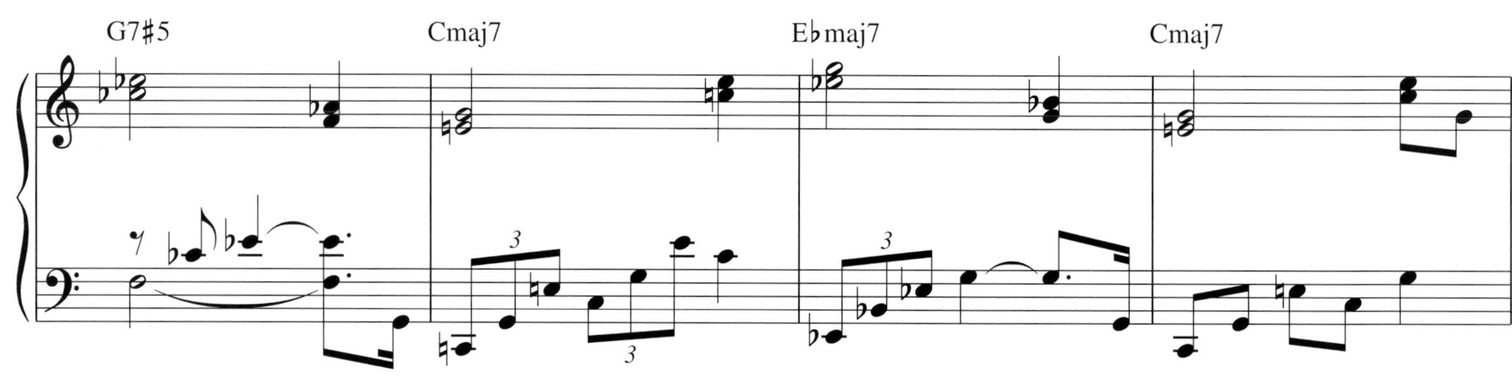

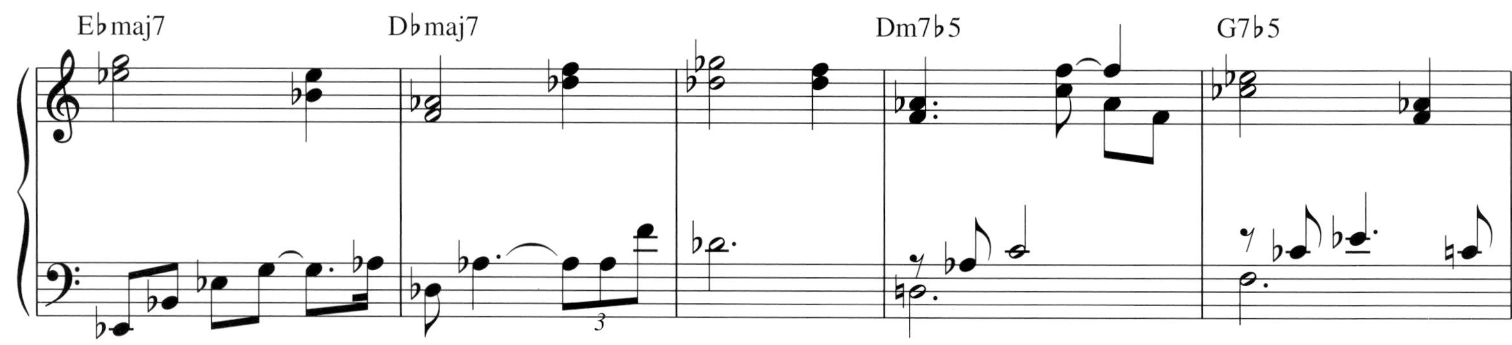

Faster
E♭6/9
G♭maj7
E♭6/9
G♭maj7
D♭maj7
Emaj7
D♭maj7
Emaj7
Cmaj7
E♭maj7
Cmaj7
E♭maj7
D♭maj7
Dm7♭5
G7♯5
Repeat ad lib. and Fade
Optional Ending
Cmaj9
E♭maj9
Cmaj9
E♭maj9
Cmaj9

RED BARON

By VINCE GUARALDI

E♭
A♭maj7
D♭9♯11
A♭maj7
D♭9♯11
Fm7
A♭/B♭
E♭maj7

F6/9
Am7
F6/9
Am7
Gm
Gm/F♯
Gm/F
Gm/E

F6/9
F
E♭

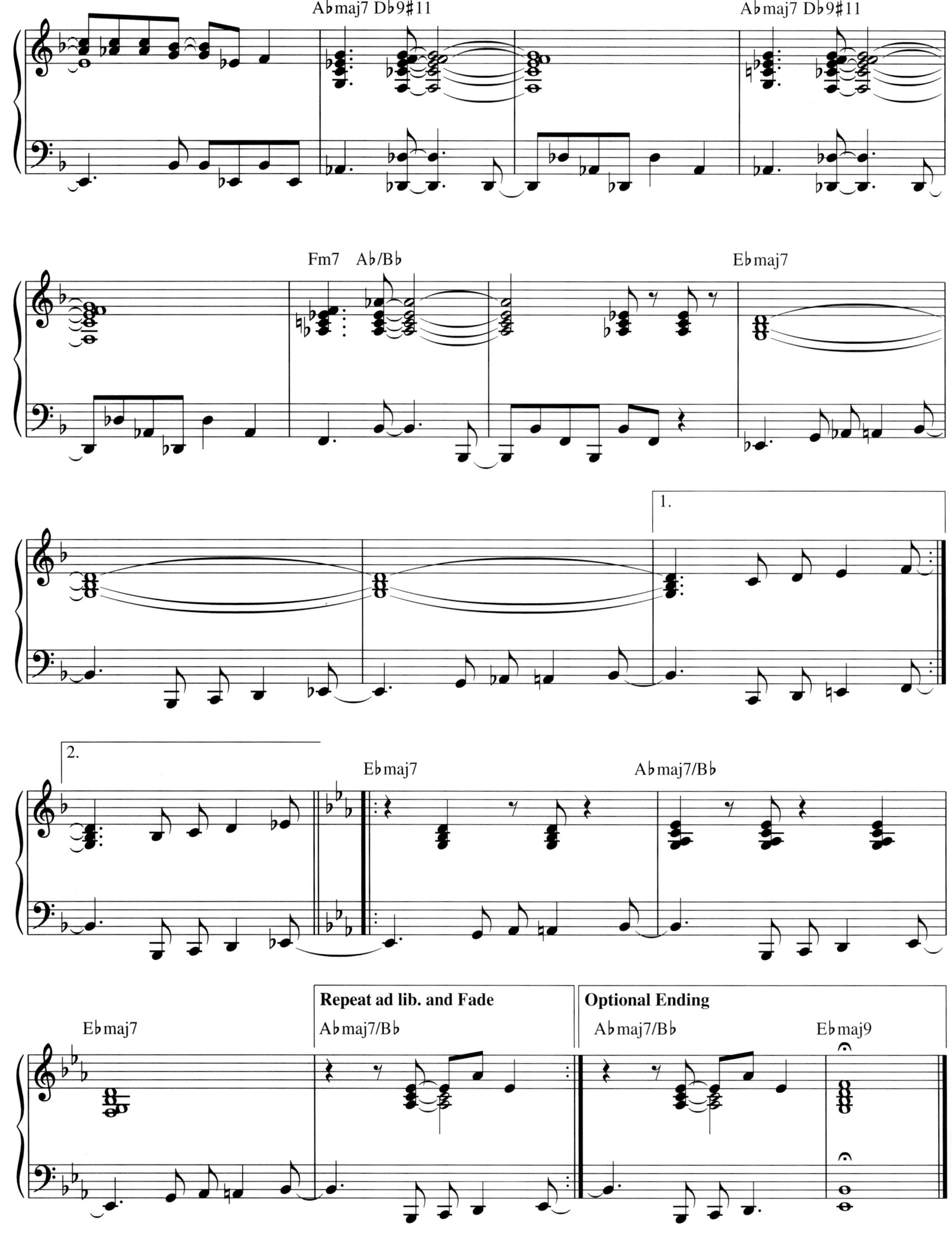
Abmaj7 Db9#11
Abmaj7 Db9#11
Fm7 Ab/Bb
Ebmaj7
1.
2.
Ebmaj7
Abmaj7/Bb
Ebmaj7
Repeat ad lib. and Fade
Abmaj7/Bb
Optional Ending
Abmaj7/Bb
Ebmaj9

SCHROEDER

By VINCE GUARALDI

Moderately

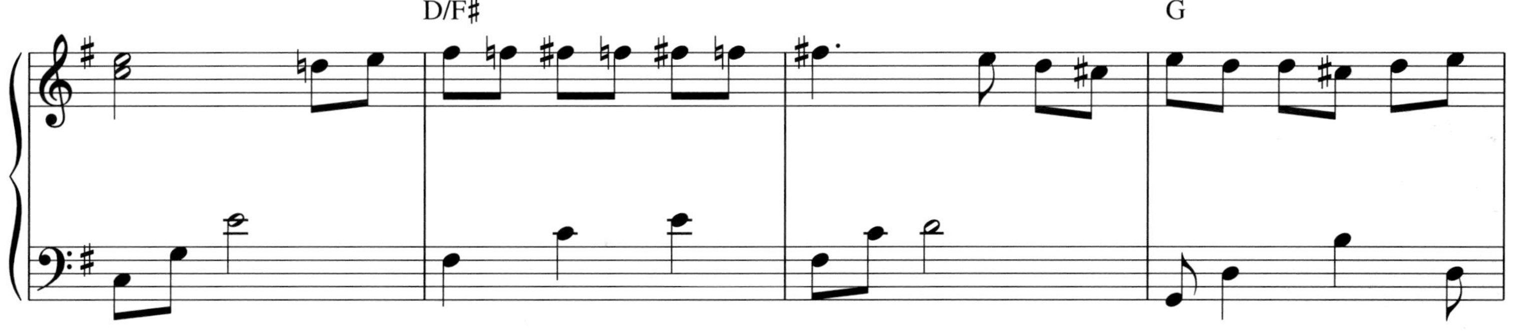

Rubato (with motion)
G
G7
C
G
D7
G
C
G
A
D
a tempo
rit.
3
G
G7
C
F#7/C#
G
F#7/C#
G
A7
D/F#
G
G7
C
G
D
G7

Freely
C
G
A7
D7/F♯
N.C.
tr
3
3
3
a tempo
G
G7
C
F♯7/C♯
G
F♯7/C♯
G
A7
D/F♯
Slightly faster
G
C
G
D
G

SKATING

By VINCE GUARALDI

Bright Jazz Waltz

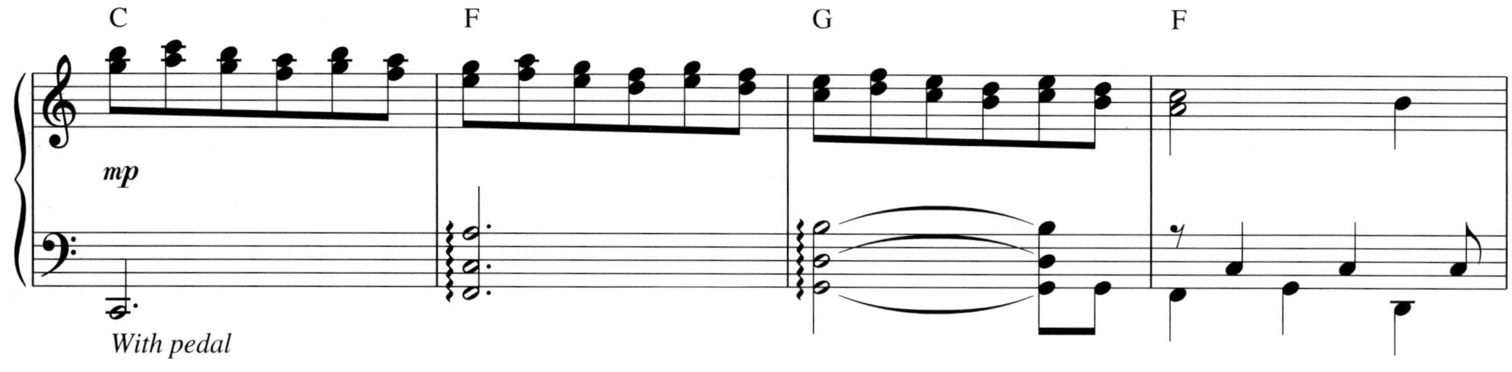

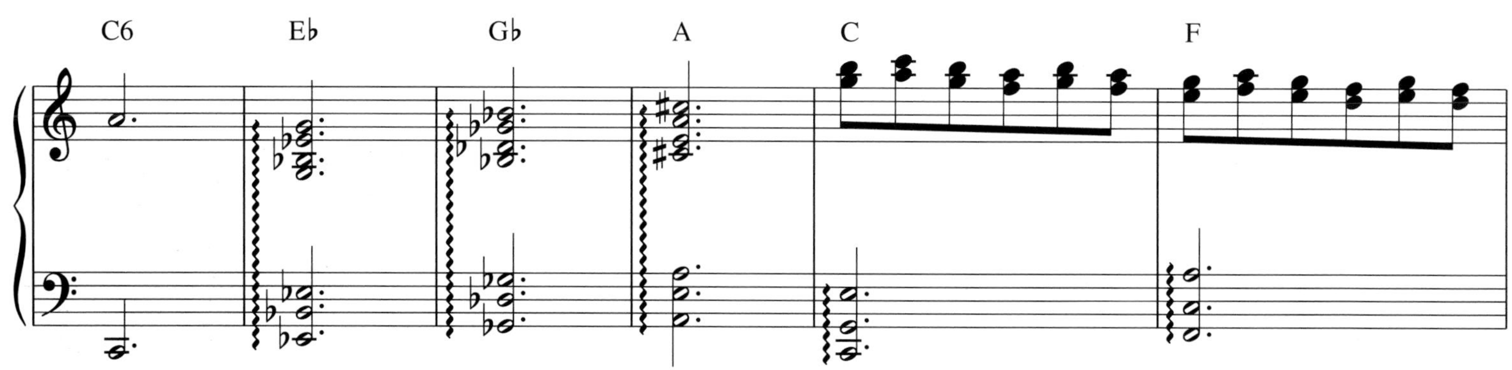

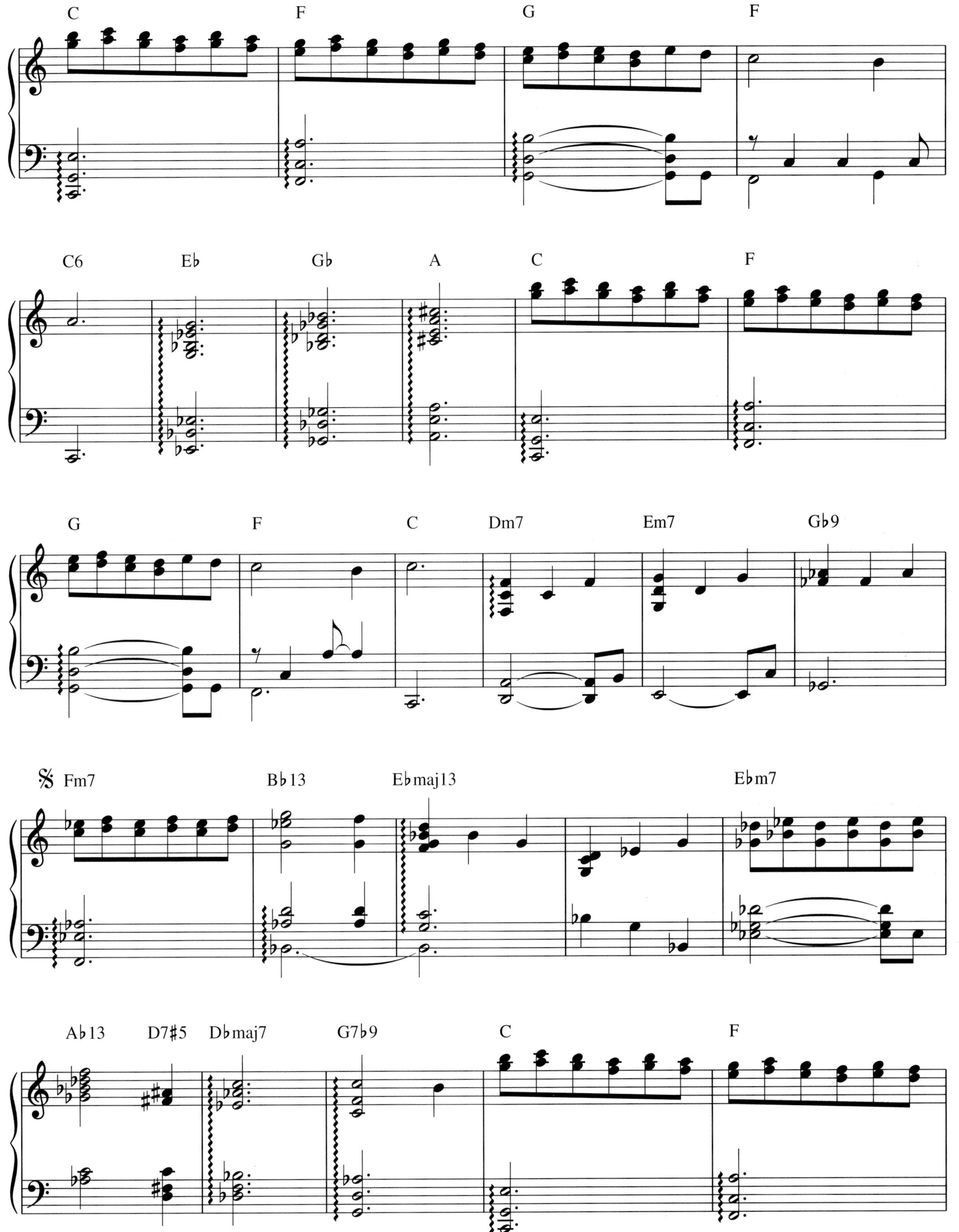
C
F
G
F
C6
E♭
G♭
A
C
F
G
F
C
Dm7
Em7
G♭9
Fm7
B♭13
E♭maj13
E♭m7
A♭13
D7♯5
D♭maj7
G7♭9
C
F

G
F
C6
E♭
G♭
A
To Coda
C
F
G
F
1.
2.
C6/9
F6/9
G6/9
F6/9
F6/9
D.S. al Coda
CODA
C
F
G
F
Repeat and Fade
Optional Ending
C6/9
F6/9
G6/9
F6/9
C6/9

SURFIN' SNOOPY

By VINCE GUARALDI

D7♭5
Dm7
G7♯5
Cmaj7
G7♯5
Cmaj7
G7♯5
Cmaj7
G7
Em7♭5
A7♯5
D7
G7sus
Em7♭5
A7sus
A7

1.
Am7
D7
G7
Cmaj7

G7sus
2.
Am7
D7
D7♭5

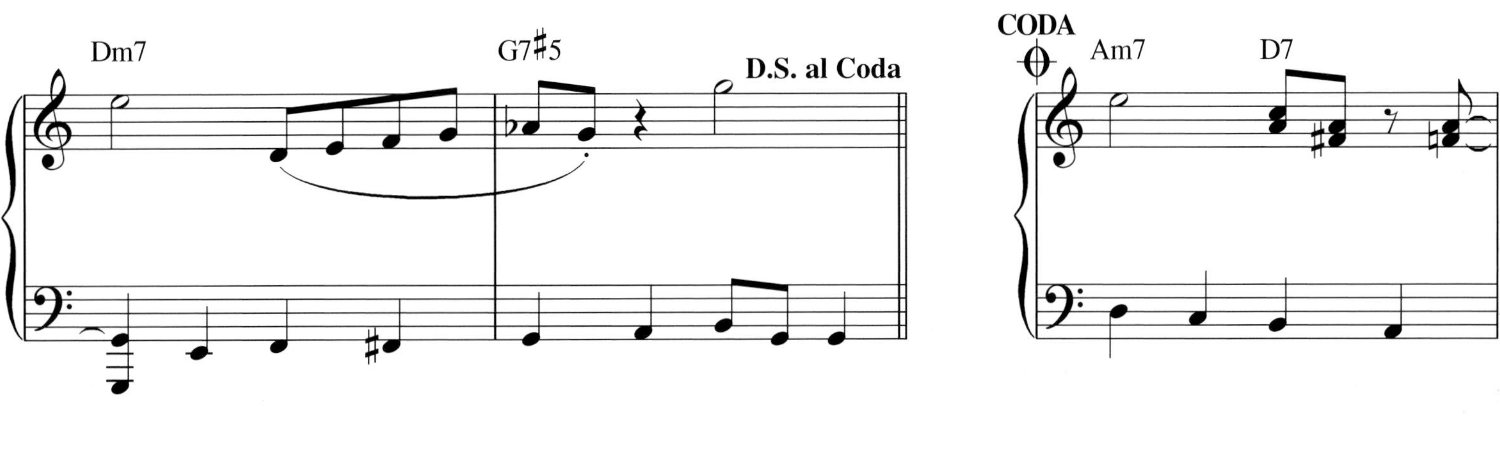
Dm7
G7♯5
D.S. al Coda
CODA
Am7
D7

G7sus
Cmaj7
Cmaj9

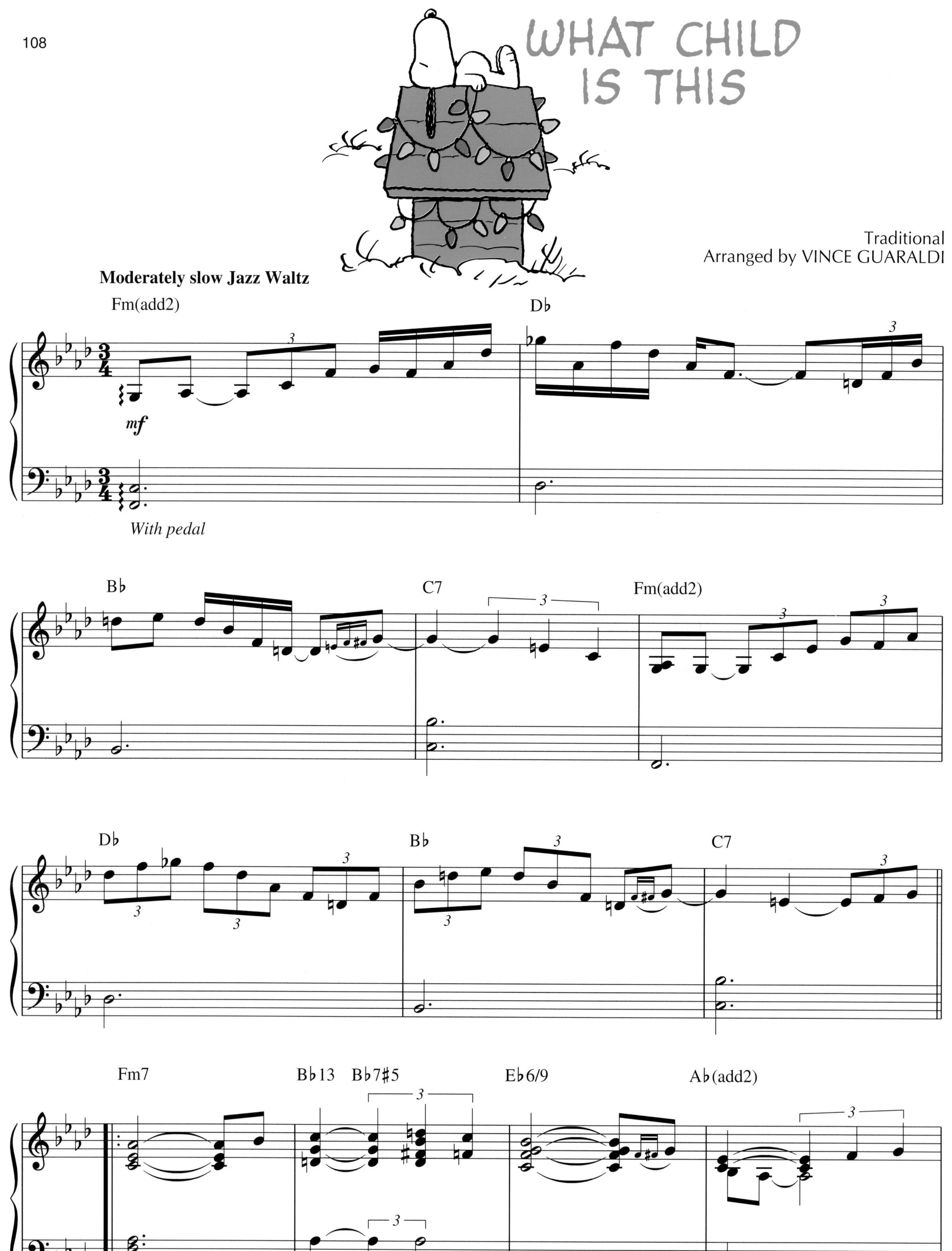
WHAT CHILD IS THIS
Traditional
Arranged by VINCE GUARALDI
Moderately slow Jazz Waltz
Fm(add2)
Db
mf
With pedal
Bb
C7
Fm(add2)
Db
Bb
C7
Fm7
Bb13
Bb7#5
Eb6/9
Ab(add2)

D♭maj7
G11♭9
G7♯5
Cm
Fm7
B♭13
B♭7♯5
E♭6/9
A♭(add2)
D♭maj7
C7
Fm(add2)
D♭
B♭
C7
Fm7
D♭
B♭
1.
C7
2.
C7

A♭maj7
Am7♭5
D7
Gm7
G7
Cm6
Fm7
B♭9
Cm6
A♭maj7
Am7♭5
D7
Gm7
G7
Cm6
D♭maj9
C7
Fm(add2)
D♭
B♭
C

Fm(add2)
Db
Bb
C
Fm6/9
Db
Bb
C
Fm(add2)
Db
Bb
C
Fm(add2)
Db
Bb
C7
Fm6/9

YOU'RE IN LOVE, CHARLIE BROWN

By VINCE GUARALDI

Db
C
F
Eb
Ab
Db
Eb13
Ab
Db/Ab
Abm7
1.
Db/Ab
2.
Db/A
Dm7b5
Dbm7
Ab(add9)/C
Bdim7
Bbm7
Eb7
Ebm7
Ab13

Dm7b5
Dbm7
Ab(add9)/C
Bdim7
Bbm7
Eb7
Bb
Adim/Bb
Ab+/Bb
Bb9
Ab
Db/Ab
Abm7
Db/Ab
Ab
Db
Eb
Db
Ab
Db

Eb
Db
C
F
Eb
Ab
Db
Eb13
To Coda
D.S. al Coda
(take repeats)
Ab
Db/Ab
Abm7
Db/Ab
CODA
Db/Ab
Ab
Db/Ab
Abm7
Db/Ab
Freely
Play 3 times
Ab(add9)

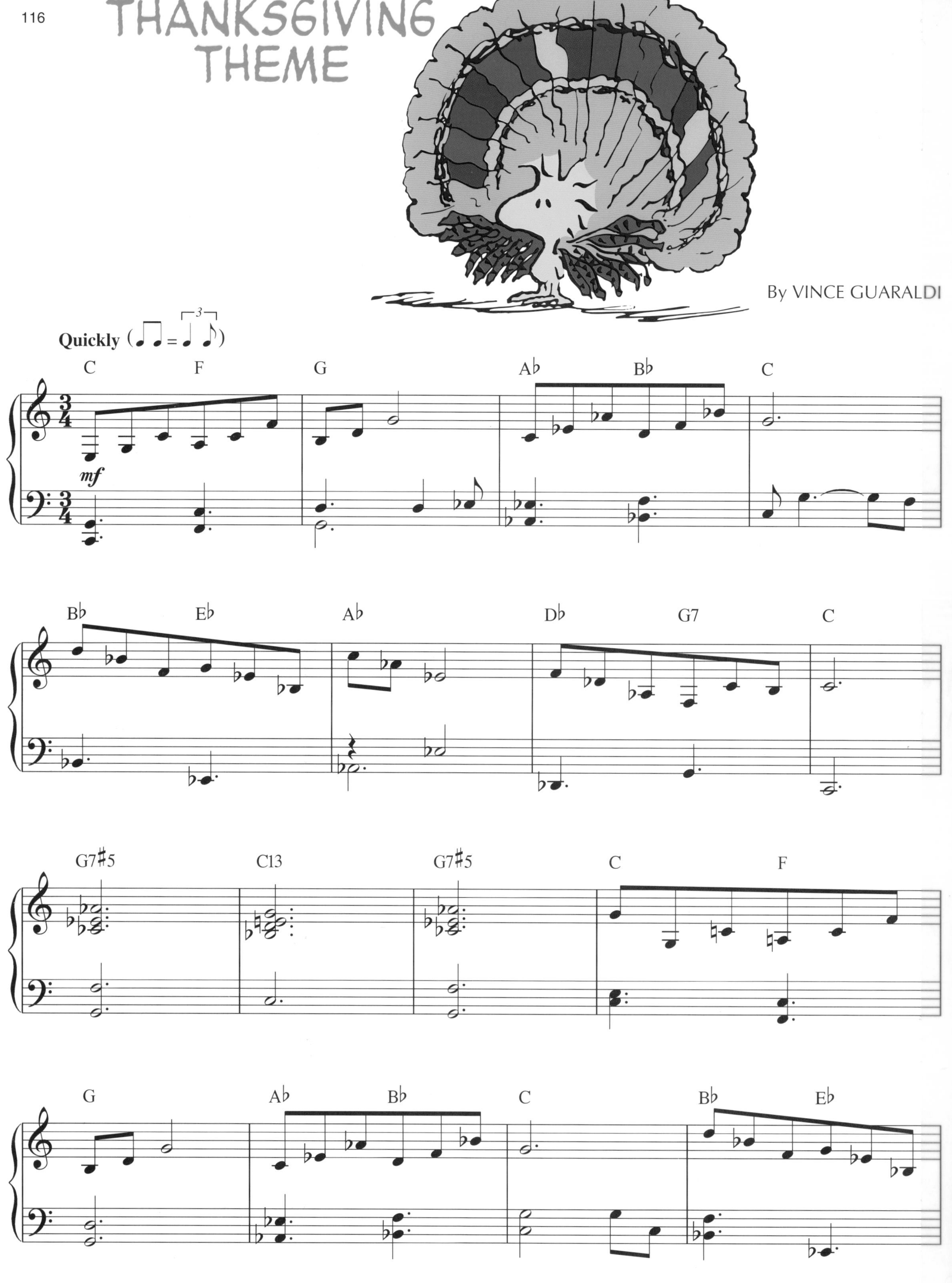
THANKSGIVING THEME
By VINCE GUARALDI
Quickly
C F G A♭ B♭ C
mf
B♭ E♭ A♭ D♭ G7 C
G7♯5 C13 G7♯5 C F
G A♭ B♭ C B♭ E♭

A♭
D♭
G7
C
G7♯5
To Coda
C13
G7♯5
G13(add4)

C
F
G
A♭
B♭
C
B♭
E♭
A♭
D♭
G7
C
G7♯5
C13
G7♯5
C6/9
F6/9
G6/9
A6
B♭maj7
Cmaj9

B♭
E♭
A♭maj7
D♭maj7
G7
Cmaj7
G7♯5
C13
1.
G7♯5
2.
G13(add4)

D.C. al Coda

CODA

C13 G7♯5 C F

G A♭ B♭ D♭ C

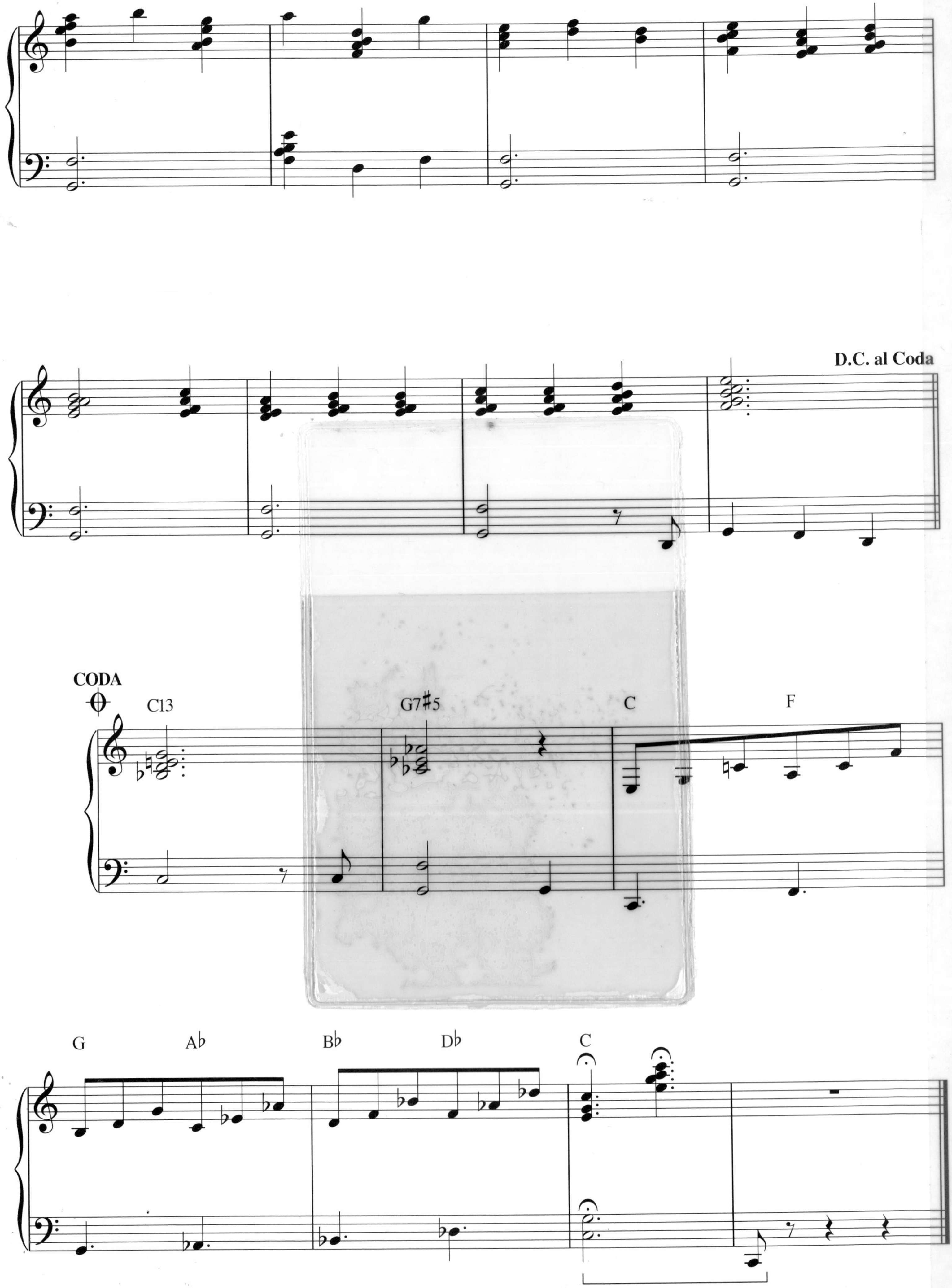